TAKUR GHAR

The SEALs and Rangers on Roberts Ridge, Afghanistan 2002

LEIGH NEVILLE

ACKNOWLEDGMENTS

Thanks to Jodi Fraser and to Kathy and Eddie Schluter for their
continued support.

DEDICATION

This work is dedicated to the seven servicemen who lost their lives
on Takur Ghar on March 3–4, 2002:

Specialist Marc A. Anderson, US Army Rangers
Technical Sergeant John A. Chapman, USAF Special Tactics
Private First Class Matthew A. Commons, US Army Rangers
Sergeant Bradley S. Crose, US Army Rangers
Senior Airman Jason D. Cunningham, USAF Special Tactics
Petty Officer First Class Nell C. Roberts, US Navy SEALs
Sergeant Philip J. Svitak, US Army 160th SOAR

AUTHOR'S NOTE

Note on weights and measures used in the text: the US military uses a
curious mix of US customary and metric measurements. Metric is used
in measurements pertaining to small arms, most support weapons and
heavier ordnance such as ground artillery (for example 7.62mm, 25mm,
or 105mm) although some weapon systems retain a US customary
measurement (notably the .50-caliber M2 Browning). Metric distance is
used to define distances between two points (100km, for example) but
altitude is measured in US customary units (for example, 500ft). To confuse
matters further, air-delivered ordnance is weighed in US customary units
(thus a 500lb JDAM), as are the weights of weapons systems. In the interest
of matching the sources and in commonality with current US military
terminology, this text follows US military protocol.

Additionally, many names of locations and individuals in Afghanistan are
spelt, and translated from Dari or Pashto into English, in multiple ways.
Wherever possible, we have followed the most common spelling available
in English.

EDITOR'S NOTE

For ease of comparison please refer to the following conversion table:

1 mile = 1.6km
1yd = 0.9m
1ft = 0.3m
1in = 2.54cm/25.4mm
1 gallon (US) = 3.8 liters
1 ton (US) = 0.9 metric tons
1lb = 0.45kg

CONTENTS

INTRODUCTION

The battle of Takur Ghar, or the battle of Roberts Ridge as it is commonly known within the US military, occurred on March 3–4, 2002, on a rugged and snow-capped mountain in southeastern Afghanistan. Takur Ghar, which roughly translates from the Pashto as "Tall Mountain," is an imposing feature of the eastern ridge of the Shahikot Valley, reaching a height of some 10,469ft above sea level. It towers over the surrounding peaks by at least 1,000ft and over the valley itself, making Takur Ghar strategically important for any military operation into the Shahikot itself. In March 2002, that fact was not lost on the US military, nor on its enemy.

The battle of Takur Ghar became perhaps the most memorable part, at least in the general public's mind, of a much larger operation known as *Anaconda*. *Anaconda* was the biggest US military air assault (meaning to insert soldiers into a hostile location by helicopters) since Vietnam, and became the largest and longest battle the US military had faced since *Desert Storm* in 1991.

Operation *Enduring Freedom*, the US military codename for operations in Afghanistan after September 11, 2001, had been a stunning success. The ruling Taliban government, who imposed a medieval form of Sharia law upon the Afghan people, had been driven from power in an unconventional campaign that had lasted some three months. The remnants of the Taliban, along with al-Qaeda and aligned foreign jihadists it harbored, were on the run. Success had been achieved through the classic Special Forces mission set: infiltrate into the target area; develop relationships with local guerrilla warlords; train, equip, and advise the local forces; and conduct unconventional warfare, supported by massive Coalition airpower.

Barely 400 "boots on the ground" had been deployed into the landlocked country, in the form of: the US Army's 5th Special Forces Group (Airborne) – the famous Green Berets; elements of the secretive Joint Special Operations Command (JSOC); operatives from the Central Intelligence Agency's (CIA) Special Activities Division (SAD) – Ground Branch; attached US Air Force Special Tactics personnel; and a handful of United Kingdom Special Forces.

Spearheaded by the CIA, Special Forces teams linked up with Afghan opposition fighters and formed what was loosely known as the Northern Alliance of anti-Taliban mujahideen fighters. The CIA and Special Forces brought with them millions of dollars in hard currency that was doled out to local warlords to buy their support. With the money, the US also bought the fighting power of the warlords' militias – often poorly trained but enthusiastic Afghan fighters, many with combat experience dating back through the Civil War of the 1990s to the Soviet–Afghan War of the 1980s.

The US also brought the world's finest close air support and strategic bombing capability into play against the Taliban and its foreign jihadist allies. Using their superb training and cutting-edge technology, the CIA and the Special Operations Forces (SOF) mentored and directed the anti-Taliban Afghan militias in a number of sweeping victories. City after city rapidly fell with thousands of Taliban fighters killed by precision guided munitions from the air. By December 2001, the Taliban were no longer an effective fighting force let alone a government, and an interim government led by Hamid Karzai was put in place ahead of elections.

As the world applauded the toppling of the Taliban regime, the enemy was regrouping in a remote valley, far from the eyes of the US military.

Two MH-47E Chinooks of the 160th SOAR launching on a mission somewhere in Afghanistan. (DOD)

ORIGINS

Into the Place of the King

The Shahikot Valley, which translates as the "Place of the King," stretches some 9km in length and is some 5km wide at its widest point. It is composed of two distinct areas, the Lower and Upper Shahikot, which run roughly parallel to each other.

In the Lower Shahikot, several imposing mountains dominate the landscape; chief amongst them is Takur Ghar at the southeast end of the valley. Farther to the northeast is Tsapare Ghar, dominating the northern entrance to the valley. On the western side of the valley is Tergul (Tir Ghol) Ghar to the northwest, again looking down on the northern entrance, and Khosa Chinah to the south, dominating the southern approach.

During the 1980s, the valley had become a sanctuary for Afghan mujahideen and their foreign jihadist comrades fighting against the might of the Soviet Union. The valley was one of three key logistics hubs for the mujahideen during the 1980s. The famed Afghan authority Lester W. Grau has established that a mujahideen commander called Malawi Nasrullah Mansoor ran the logistics node in the valley and invited foreign jihadists travelling into Afghanistan to base themselves in the Lower Shahikot to fight their jihad against the Soviets.

Mansoor soon fortified the valley, digging trench systems and building caves and bunkers into the ridges, many of which would be put to deadly effect some 20 years later. After the withdrawal of the Soviets, Mansoor became a provincial governor before being assassinated in 1993. His pro-Taliban son took over the valley in the wake of his father's death and was soon inviting the foreign fighters of Usama bin Laden's al-Qaeda to use the Shahikot as a logistics base, in much the same fashion as his father had once done with the "Afghan Arabs" in the 1980s.

Opposite

A map displaying the provinces and principal cities of Afghanistan in 2002. Of particular note is Paktia province to the east along the border with Pakistan showing the location of Gardez and Khowst, both central to the story of Takur Ghar (also note the distance from Bagram to the north). Also note Tarnak Farms, further to the south, in Zabol province. Tarnak Farms was both a former training camp for al-Qaeda and home to bin Laden, and a Coalition live-fire range where half of Captain Nate Self's Rangers were training when the March 4 battle occurred.

6

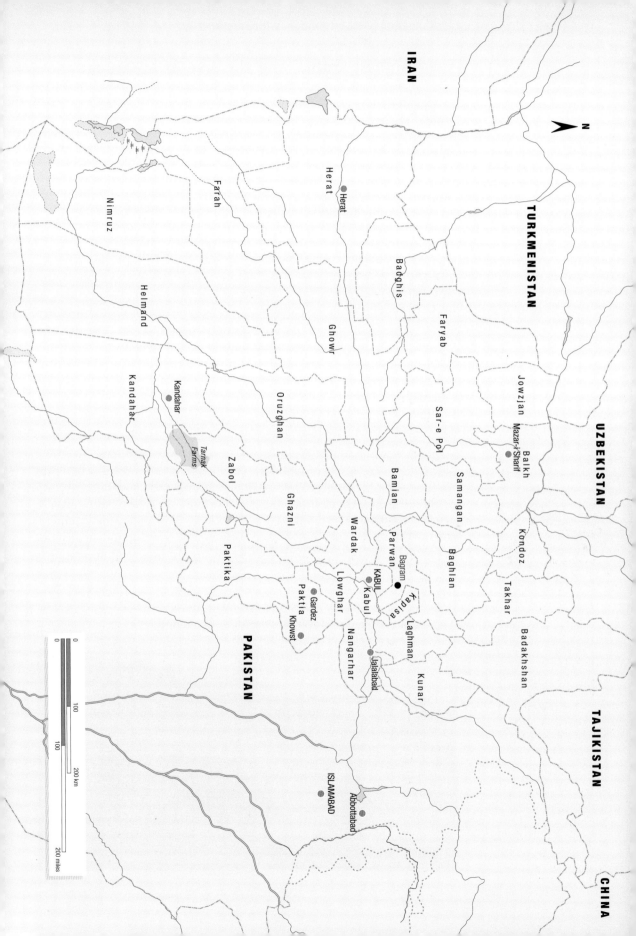

The "Afghan Arabs" and the rise of al-Qaeda

The "Afghan Arabs" were a collection of Arabic volunteers who journeyed to Afghanistan in the 1980s to fight jihad ("holy war") against the Soviet invaders. Financed primarily by Saudi sheikhs, the "Afghan Arabs" eventually numbered some 30,000 fighters. Although disliked by many Afghan mujahideen, the "Afghan Arabs" assisted in eventually forcing the withdrawal of Soviet forces from the country.

Among these volunteers was a young Saudi millionaire, Usama bin Laden. Bin Laden established a guesthouse for foreign insurgents, which came to be known as al-Qaeda ("The Base"). From these humble beginnings he organized a personal force of "Afghan Arabs" who pledged fealty to the young Saudi. At the end of the Soviet–Afghan War, bin Laden returned to Saudi Arabia for a short time before being forced out by the Saudi Government, and moving on to Sudan.

Al-Qaeda and the jihadist networks developed further in Sudan and Yemen until eventually Bin Laden returned to Afghanistan in 1996, after pressure from the American Government led to his expulsion from Sudan. Upon his return to Afghanistan, he found strong allies in the Taliban. The Taliban gained prominence in 1994, during the bitter civil war wracking the country. The Talibs (religious students) were led by Mullah Omar, a charismatic Pashtun who garnered much popular support due to his stance against the warlords and their opium trade.

With al-Qaeda's assistance (bin Laden recruited a large "Afghan Arab" force known as Brigade 55 to fight against the anti-Taliban Northern Alliance, or Shura Nazar), the Taliban won the civil war in 1996 and imposed their brutal interpretation of Sharia law. By this time, bin Laden and al-Qaeda had begun to export their fight to the "Far Enemy," the United States, and its allies. Responsible for bombings in East Africa, Kuwait, and finally the attack on the USS *Cole* in Yemen, al-Qaeda was fast becoming the principal asymmetrical threat to the West. The group cemented this reputation with the attack on September 11, 2001. After the terrorist hijackings, the United States asked the Taliban government to hand over bin Laden; they refused, and Operation *Enduring Freedom* was launched.

An iconic early image of Special Forces in Afghanistan riding into battle on horseback alongside their Afghan allies of the Northern Alliance. (DOD)

INITIAL STRATEGY

Enduring Freedom

Military operations began on the night of October 6, 2001 with the coalition's Operation *Crescent Wind*. US ground forces, in the form of operatives from the CIA's SAD – Ground Branch, had arrived in Afghanistan 15 days after the events of September 11 and were busy striking deals with Afghan warlords. Carrying millions of dollars of US currency, the SAD operatives bought the support of the Afghan militias opposed to the Taliban. By October 19, the first US Army Special Forces Operational Detachment Alpha (ODA) teams were on the ground linking up with the CIA "pilot teams" and their newly recruited Afghan allies.

The Special Forces ODAs, assisted by small numbers of JSOC (Joint Special Operations Command) and UK Special Forces operators, began an unconventional warfare campaign against the Taliban and al-Qaeda. Deploying their SOFLAMs (Special Operations Forces Laser Markers) the ODAs guided in precision close air support from US Air Force, US Navy, and Royal Air Force strike aircraft and bombers. This "magic" created awe amongst their Afghan recruits and resulted in an increase in battlefield confidence, if not competence. In at least one notable case, this 21st-century technology was matched with an 18th-century cavalry charge, as B-52s supported Afghan horsemen (the battle of Bai Beche, November 2001). Soon, the Taliban-held cities began falling.

The campaign, a classic Special Forces mission, lasted 49 days and resulted in the toppling of the Taliban Government and the capture of all major population centers. Conventional forces from the 15th Marine Expeditionary Unit and the 10th Mountain and 101st Airborne divisions soon arrived to support the SOF vanguard. The Taliban and their al-Qaeda allies were in shock and disarray and many retreated to the south and east of the country. With NATO support, the International Security Assistance Force (ISAF) was deployed to begin the task of reconstruction.

Members of the 2nd Battalion, 187th Infantry conduct a dismounted sweep and clear during Operation *Mountain Lion*, a follow-up operation to *Anaconda* in April 2002. This clearly shows the type of terrain Coalition forces were forced to navigate during *Anaconda*. (US Army)

OCTOBER 6, 2001

Military operations in Afghanistan start

Special Operations Forces

SOF were organized into five individual task forces with specific roles and responsibilities: Joint Special Operations Task Force – North (JSOTF–N), known as Task Force Dagger; Joint Special Operations Task Force – South (JSOTF–S), known as Task Force K-Bar; Task Force Sword; The Joint Inter Agency Task Force – Counter Terrorism (JIATF–CT), known as Task Force Bowie; and Task Force 64.

Task Force Dagger was based around the US Army's 5th Special Forces Group and provided the principal force who overthrew the Taliban and were instrumental in developing early counterinsurgency efforts throughout the war-devastated nation. Task Force K-Bar was initially manned by US Navy SEAL (Sea, Air, Land) Teams and elements of the 3rd Special Forces Group. Task Force K-Bar was also in command of the majority of Coalition SOF such as the Canadian Joint Task Force 2, the New Zealand Special Air Service Group, and the Danish Army Jaegerkorpset (Hunter Corps). K-Bar was primarily tasked with both long-range Special Reconnaissance (SR) and Sensitive Site Exploitation (SSE).

Task Force Sword, later renamed Task Force 11, was an independent command of JSOC, with the sole purpose of hunting Taliban and al-Qaeda High Value Targets (HVTs). Sword was manned by rotating squadrons from the Army and Navy JSOC Special Mission Units (SMUs). Task Force Bowie was established as an intelligence fusion cell, gathering and disseminating actionable intelligence product to both the conventional forces and SOF task forces. Finally, Task Force 64 was the title given to the Australian Special Forces Task Group from the Special Air Service Regiment (SASR). The Australians were tasked with specialist long-range reconnaissance missions, enabled by the fact that SASR were the only Coalition SOF to bring their own vehicles into theater.

Advanced Force Operations

Advanced Force Operations (AFO) was a small element that operated under the control of Task Force Sword, the JSOC task force, which was renamed Task Force 11 in late 2001, commanding all "black" SOF in the Afghanistan theater of war. Initially when AFO was deployed, it numbered no more than 45 operators, primarily drawn from the ranks of the Army's Tier One SMUs, the 1st Special Forces Operational Detachment – Delta but including reconnaissance/sniper specialists from JSOC's Navy SEAL Tier One SMU, the Naval Special Warfare Development Group (DEVGRU), and attached Combat Controllers and Pararescue Jumpers from the USAF's 24th Special Tactics Squadron (STS).

Delta had already had their B Squadron operational in Afghanistan in October 2001 conducting wide-ranging mobility operations in their Pinzgauer Special Operations Vehicles. They had also carried out one of the first offensive combat operations of the war in October 2001 when they air assaulted by MH-47E Chinooks into a walled compound outside of Kandahar, known as Objective Gecko, in search of Mullah Omar, the one-eyed cleric who led the Taliban militia. Rangers from the 1st Battalion, 75th Rangers, provided a force-protection outer cordon whilst Delta conducted the clearance and search. They didn't find Mullah Omar, but they did run into a large number of Taliban who responded quickly to the arrival of helicopters.

A vicious firefight erupted until an on-station AC-130 Spectre gunship provided precision fire support to allow the operators and Rangers to break contact and exfiltrate. The landing gear of one MH-47E was damaged in the hasty extraction, leading to predictable Taliban claims that they had downed a helicopter. A plan to leave a stay-behind party of Delta operators in a covert observation post (OP) after the raid was not surprisingly scrapped. Media coverage focused on the publicized Ranger combat drop on Objective Rhino whilst the JSOC operation at Gecko remained virtually unknown.

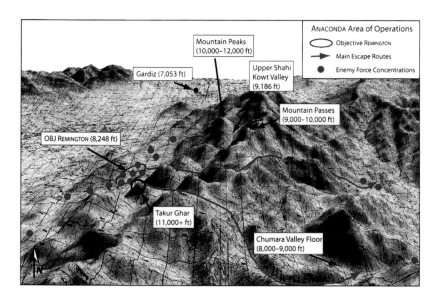

A US military briefing slide showing the Operation *Anaconda* Area of Operations. Note projected enemy locations in the Lower Shahikot and the expected "rat line" escape routes covered by observation posts from Task Force K-Bar and Task Force 64. (US Army)

An Australian SASR reconnaissance patrol from Task Force 64 in the brutal weather that afflicted all of the recon teams from AFO, Task Force K-Bar, and Task Force 64. The Australians are readying a Perentie Long Range Patrol Vehicle, a 6×6 Land Rover based design unique to the SASR. (Australian DOD)

DECEMBER 2001

Many mujahideen escape from battle of Tora Bora into Shahikot Valley

Small numbers of operators had also been working with the "pilot teams" of CIA SAD and 5th Special Forces Group personnel coordinating the war effort with the Northern and Eastern Alliance (and developing a plan for a Delta hostage rescue of several kidnapped non-governmental organization workers, which was eventually not required as they were released under a deal with Northern Alliance forces). These elements were joined in early December 2001 by a second Delta squadron (A Squadron) that hunted "HVT-1" himself – Usama bin Laden – in the mountains of Tora Bora.

AFO's operators were split between AFO South and AFO North, with a headquarters element based at Bagram within Task Force Bowie but reporting directly to Task Force 11. Task Force Bowie was led by Brigadier General Gary Harrell, a highly respected and experienced former commander of Delta, who worked for General Tommy Franks, the Central Command (CENTCOM) commander in charge of Operation *Enduring Freedom*. Bowie was designated as the in-theater intelligence "shop" with representatives from many government agencies (known to the military as OGA, for Other Government Agency) and from both conventional and SOF units.

Task Force 11 also had other DEVGRU SEALs (known as Task Force Blue) and Rangers from the 1st Battalion of the 75th Rangers (known as Task Force Red), supported by the aviators of the 160th Special Operations Aviation Regiment (160th SOAR, otherwise known as the Nightstalkers or Task Force Brown), deployed to Bagram as an assault element should actionable intelligence be received on the location of any of the high value targets on the Task Force "kill/capture" list.

Task Force 11 was commanded by the USAF's Brigadier General Gregory Trebon, based on Masirah Island, some 1,600km away from the battlespace. Trebon was vastly experienced in special-operations aviation, but had little operational experience commanding SOF ground elements. Some officers in JSOC felt that Colonel Jim Schwitters, Delta's commander, or

Captain Joe Kernan, the DEVGRU commander, should instead have been commanding the Task Force – both these men had operational experience and understood the units and tactics intimately. Trebon, and his superior Major General Dell Dailey, head of JSOC, were keen to rotate Delta out and replace them with DEVGRU teams as they felt that JSOC would be the most important command in the newly announced "Global War on Terror" (GWOT) and thus didn't want any one unit "burning out."

Delta's A Squadron had already been sent back to Fort Bragg, North Carolina, earlier than expected and Dailey and Trebon instead ordered DEVGRU squadrons into the Afghan theater, leaving Delta's undeployed C Squadron frustrated and back at Bragg. These decisions had already caused friction between Trebon, Dailey, and the on-the-ground Delta contingent, frictions which would ultimately but indirectly lead to the battle of Takur Ghar.

A pre-mission briefing to senior officers, explaining the concept of operations for Operation *Anaconda*. (US Army)

AFO was commanded by Lieutenant Colonel Pete Blaber, a former Ranger and veteran Delta officer, and were tasked to be the "eyes and ears" of the Coalition forces in Afghanistan. They were instructed by General Tommy Franks to "get some men out into the frontier to figure out what's going on" (Blaber 2008: 204). Blaber and his AFO teams needed no further prompting.

All of the Delta and DEVGRU operators assigned to AFO had been handpicked and were the elite within an elite – the sniper, surveillance, and reconnaissance specialists within their respective units. Their task was to blend in with the locals, develop intelligence leads in the field, and conduct special reconnaissance on the targets they developed.

Into the Shahikot

In early 2002, AFO analysts working hand in glove with their CIA and Special Forces compatriots and Harrell's Task Force Bowie began seeing intelligence indications that a large number of foreign fighters – "Afghan Arabs" from al-Qaeda, plus Uzbeks, Tajiks, and Chechens from the Islamic Movement of Uzbekistan (IMU) – and Afghan Taliban were hunkered down in the relative security of the Lower Shahikot Valley in eastern Afghanistan.

A 5th Special Forces reconnaissance patrol conducted by ODA 594 in late January 2002 provided the first indications. As they carried out a reconnaissance in the region of Zurmat District and Tergul Ghar in the Shahikot, their AMF (Afghan Militia Force) warned them against advancing any farther. ODA 594's reporting reached Bowie and AFO and they began looking carefully at the Lower Shahikot Valley.

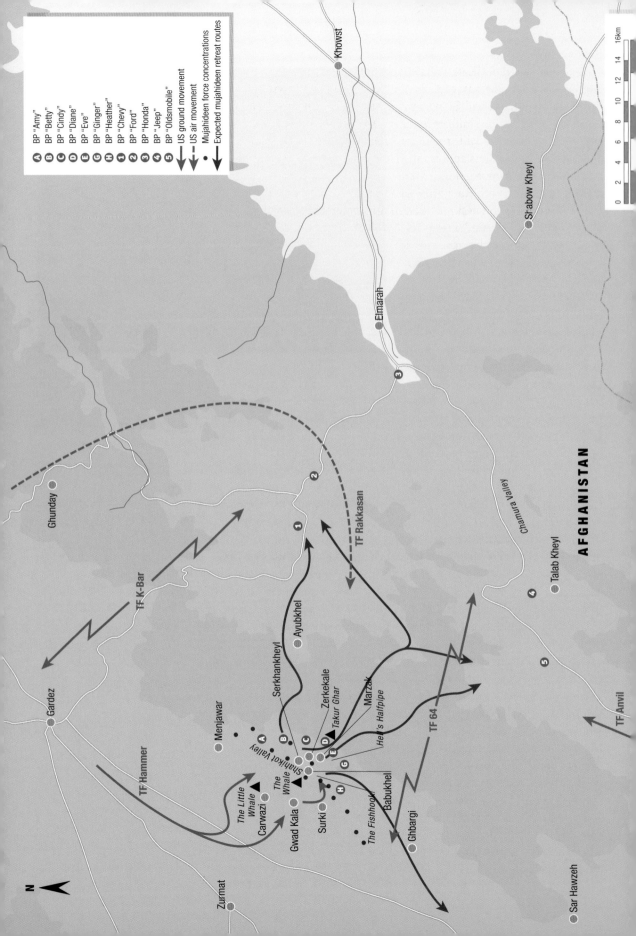

N

16km
0 2 4 6 8 10 12 14

Khowst

Sr·abow Kheyl

Elmarah

3

Ghunday

2

TF Rakkasan

TF K-Bar

1

Gardez

Chamura Valley

TF/Anvil

Talab Kheyl

4

5

Ayubkhel

Serkhankheyl

Zerkekale

Marzak

TF Hammer

Menjawar

A

B

C

D *Takur Ghar*

E *Hel's Halfpipe*

G

Shahikot Valley

The Little Whale

The Whale

Carwazi

Gwad Kala

Surki

H

The Fishhook

Babukhel

TF 64

Ghbargi

Zurmat

Sar Hawzeh

AFGHANISTAN

The intelligence indicated that enemy fighters were living in the villages of Serkhankheyl and Marzak, both located on the eastern approach. Overlooking these villages were Tergul Ghar to the west (soon nicknamed "The Whale" by US planners due to its similarity to a terrain feature at the National Training Center at Fort Irwin, California) and Takur Ghar to the south of the villages.

Many enemy fighters appeared to have fled to the valley after the defeat at Tora Bora. At Tora Bora, the CIA and Delta squadron commander requested a battalion of the 75th Ranger Regiment to be deployed to block the passes into Pakistan. The request was denied amid political fears of increasing the US military "footprint" in Afghanistan. Al-Qaeda and Taliban fighters managed to escape the aerial bombardment through bribing local AMF commanders and declaring a false truce allegedly to discuss surrender conditions. They instead used this ruse to slip away.

Some al-Qaeda, IMU, and Taliban crossed the border into Pakistan whilst the Americans' main target, bin Laden, appears to have hidden in Jalalabad for a short time before, according to respected al-Qaeda authority Peter Bergen, retreating into the mountains of Kunar province. Bin Laden eventually crossed into Pakistan and settled in a custom-built compound in Abbottabad where he was famously located and killed by DEVGRU in May 2011 on Operation *Neptune Spear*.

As the intelligence mounted on the suspected enemy concentration in the Lower Shahikot Valley, AFO began developing options for inserting personnel into observation posts to conduct both environmental reconnaissance and pattern-of-life surveillance. An environmental reconnaissance is carried out to understand the terrain that forces may encounter – for example, the difficulty in traversing certain mountain trails, the amount and depth of snow in a given area, the availability of water sources, or the general weather and climate. It is defined as "operations conducted to collect and report critical hydrographic, geological, and meteorological information" (US DOD 2003: 5) by the US military. Broadly speaking, it is gaining an understanding of the environmental factors in the target area that may impact upon military operations.

Pattern-of-life surveillance entails maintaining covert surveillance over an area of interest to develop an understanding of that area and its inhabitants. This is generally a longer-term special reconnaissance mission as time is required to monitor and understand the atmospherics of the target location. Pattern-of-life surveillance allows operators and analysts to spot when something changes in the area of interest – for example, on a certain day the villagers take food into the hills, is it to feed insurgents (as it was on *Anaconda*) or are they simply having a community picnic?

For the AFO teams, it meant a lot of cold, backbreaking work infiltrating the Shahikot covertly. Blaber made the call early in the planning phase that "there will be no direct helicopter infiltrations of AFO teams anywhere near the valley" (Blaber 2008: 227) to ensure AFO didn't spook their quarry. He felt that heliborne insertions made it impossible to surprise the enemy, giving forewarning of the operation and that the tactic limited opportunities for the teams to develop superior methods of infiltrating a target area.

Opposite

A map of the immediate battlespace of Operation Anaconda based on contemporary US military maps. The air assault route of Task Force Rakkasan and the proposed ground assault route of Task Force Hammer can be seen along with the observation posts maintained by the special operators of Task Force 64 to the south and K-Bar to the north. The outer-lying blocking positions to the east were designed to engage any mujahideen elements that managed to escape the initial encirclement of the valley and head toward Pakistan.

A Polaris ATV ridden by a Special Forces soldier prepares to drive up the ramp of a CH-47D Chinook. This was how the JULIET AFO team extracted the valley on their specially adapted Polaris ATVs. (US Air Force)

Instead, AFO chose to conduct vehicle recons of the routes into and around the valley in local 4WD Toyota vehicles and at night on specially adapted Polaris all-terrain vehicles (ATVs). These ATVs were modified by unit mechanics with infrared headlights, GPS receivers, and suppressed exhausts. They also sent two teams of highly experienced Delta operators from their squadron's Reconnaissance and Surveillance Troop into the area surrounding the Shahikot to conduct the environmental recons.

These two teams, codenamed JULIET and INDIA, with five and three operators respectively assigned, climbed high into the mountains and gorges of the Shahikot, often in the most extreme weather conditions, to gain an appreciation of the area of operations. Their vital intelligence was fed back to the AFO teams and would prove invaluable once Operation *Anaconda* was launched.

General Franks was reading the AFO daily situation reports and CIA intelligence and became convinced that an operation needed to be mounted to destroy what appeared to be a sizable enemy presence in the Lower Shahikot. Franks believed the time was right to deploy conventional forces into what could well become a large-scale, and decisive, battle with the Taliban and al-Qaeda remnants.

An initial planning meeting was held at a 5th Special Forces Group safe house with representatives of the Special Forces from Task Force Dagger, the CIA, the AFO, and staff officers from the conventional units assigned – the 1st and 2nd Battalions of the 187th Infantry Regiment (1-187th and 2-187th) from the storied 101st Airborne, known as the "Rakkasans" (from a Japanese term loosely meaning "falling down umbrella man" used to describe their original role as parachute troops), and the 1st Battalion of the 87th Infantry Regiment (1-87th) of the 10th Mountain Division. Neither unit had thus far been committed to any significant combat operations and both were understandably keen to see action. As the Rakkasans were trained and equipped as air assault infantry, they also understandably began to develop an airmobile option for the attack into the Shahikot. Blaber made his point early at the meeting, backed by strong reluctance from AFO, Special Forces, and CIA, concerning the idea of landing troops in the valley by helicopter:

> Understand that because of the terrain and altitude, there are only two air corridors the helicopters can use to fly into the valley, and you should assume both will be covered by heavy weapons. Remember that every enemy on the planet expects the US military to attack using helicopters; this enemy will be no different. The time it will take the large, lumbering Chinooks to brake, flare, hover, and then land will make you highly vulnerable to the enemy's antiaircraft weapons. (Blaber 2008: 241)

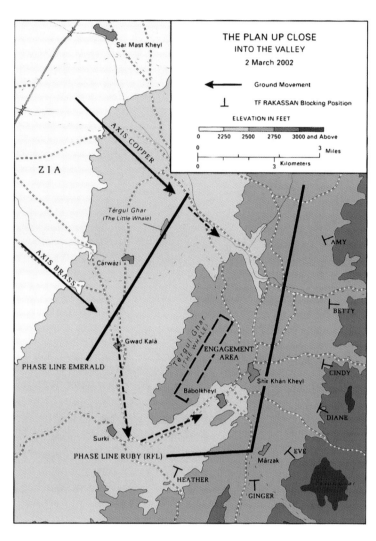

A US military briefing map showing the original plan featuring the main axis of attack of Task Force Hammer and the location of all proposed blocking positions to be manned by Task Force Rakkasan. (US Army)

If any air assault was to be conducted, the SOF argued that Task Force Rakkasan should land at offset HLZs (Helicopter Landing Zones) in the heights of the Upper Shahikot and move in over the mountains to preserve at least some surprise and to hit the enemy from a direction they were not expecting.

Task Force Rakkasan held the view that inserting into the mountains would limit the amount of equipment and supplies the soldiers could carry due to the increased altitude, and slow their progress by forcing movement through snow-covered, difficult terrain. Additionally, an insertion into the mountains would potentially deprive the conventional forces of air cover from their AH-64As as the altitude would be too high for the attack helicopters to operate in.

Despite SOF's reluctance with regard to the air assault the plan to use the helicopters to land in the valley solidified. In simple terms, the concept of operations was for Task Force Rakkasan to air assault into the valley in CH-47D Chinooks supported by six AH-64A Apache gunships and occupy blocking positions (BPs) along the eastern ridgeline of the Shahikot.

Task Force Rakkasan prepare to board their CH-47D Chinooks for a dry run of the air assault into the Lower Shahikot. (US Army)

Apart from organic 60mm mortars and a single 120mm mortar tube, Task Force Rakkasan would be fully reliant on the attached AH-64As and Air Force, Marine, and Navy fast air for fire support.

The Chinooks were used rather than the small UH-60 Blackhawks as the lowest HLZ was at a height of 8,500ft, an altitude that a fully loaded Blackhawk would simply not be able to attain (one UH-60 was employed as a C2 platform for the 10th Mountain battalion staff but only carried a reduced complement of half-a-dozen individuals). The conventional troops would act as the "anvil," manning seven BPs along the eastern ridges and destroying enemy forces fleeing from the "hammer."

The "hammer" was based around a Special Forces force element built around some 450 Afghan militia fighters led by Commander Zia Lodin, and was considered the main effort. Lodin's AMF, suitably code named Task Force Hammer, would enter the valley from the northern entrance in a mix of locally procured vehicles after a pre-planned aerial bombardment of key enemy positions identified by the AFO teams and other Coalition SR teams. They would then assault through the villages of Serkhankheyl and Marzak where the intelligence indicated the enemy was concentrated and force fleeing enemy forces into the BPs.

Lodin's militia were somewhat amusingly termed "Tier One Pashtuns" by the Special Forces due to their ability to learn from training and advice provided by the SF and their eagerness to take the battle to the Taliban and al-Qaeda. His forces, with ODAs 372 and 594 and a small team of AFO, CIA, and SASR liaisons attached, would travel south from Gardez and turn west, attacking toward the village of Serkhankheyl and the towering Tergul Ghar known as "The Whale."

Two other locally recruited Afghan forces – Kamel Khan's AMF (supported by ODA 392 and 571) and Zakim Khan's forces (supported by ODAs 381 and 542) – were designated Task Force Anvil and were tasked with establishing an outer cordon to stop any enemy "squirters" from escaping into Pakistan. Zakim Khan's fighters would establish BPs at the southern end of the valley whilst Kamel Khan's AMF would drive from Khowst and man an outer perimeter to the east.

The Special Forces leadership were concerned that Task Force Rakkasan would be landing just short of their objectives and in front of the Afghan forces of Zia Lodin and felt that a friendly fire incident was inevitable. The commanders of their attached ODAs even went to the extent of parading around an American combat engineer dressed in full "battle rattle" so that they could hopefully identify friendly forces in the confusion of battle. Nothing could be done to eliminate the possibility of Task Force Rakkasan soldiers firing on the Afghans who dressed and were equipped in a similar manner to their Taliban opponents.

If a HVT was positively located during *Anaconda*, all offensive operations were to be stopped and conventional forces were tasked to place a cordon around the location of the HVT, ensuring that no enemy could escape or be reinforced. They would then await the arrival of Task Force 11's direct action assault elements that would conduct the actual capture.

The Task Force Blue SEALs and the Task Force Red Ranger element would fly up from Bagram in their designated Nightstalker helicopters with flying times estimated at roughly an hour. The agreed procedure was a ridiculous requirement when

considering the highly trained veteran operators from both black SOF and white SOF already in the immediate Area of Operations (AO). Additionally, the idea of halting all offensive operations in the middle what could be a major battle was likewise ill-considered at the least.

Infantrymen of Task Force Rakkasan conduct dry runs, practising their building clearance drills using string on the ground to mark out the boundaries of the buildings. (US Army)

An Air Force Combat Controller attached to a Special Forces ODA guides in Coalition air strikes, using his SOFLAM laser designator to mark the target for the laser-guided bombs. (DOD)

The enemy

Further intelligence developed by Task Force Bowie, the AFO, and the CIA reported that the Taliban and foreign fighters had forced the local Afghans from the villages on the valley floor with few civilians remaining. It was also ascertained that a wanted Taliban commander, Jalaluddin Haqani, a seasoned veteran of the Soviet–Afghan War and once supported by Western intelligence agencies, was in overall military command of the valley.

Additionally, Islamic Movement of Uzbekistan deputy leader Tahir Yuldashev was present on the ground and in command of IMU forces in the area. Saifur Rahman Mansoor was allegedly in charge of the Taliban elements within the Valley. There were even indicators that other HVTs, including bin Laden, may have been resident in the valley.

The noted Afghanistan specialist, Lester Grau, believes there were initially some 600 estimated enemy fighters in the valley, which tallies with other credible sources. Coalition intelligence estimates pre-*Anaconda* of 150 enemy indicates that they had significantly underestimated opposition strength in the valley. Colonel Mulholland of the 5th Special Forces Group later commented, "I knew in my gut that there were more than a few hundred" (Briscoe et al. 2003: 281).

These mujahideen forces were deployed in what appeared to be a "caste" system of sorts with little direct coordination between the "castes" – Pete Blaber recounts that al-Qaeda and the "Afghan Arabs" were considered (by themselves) as the top tier, with the Uzbeks and Chechens of the IMU next down, and finally the Afghan Taliban on the lowest rung of the ladder. A disgruntled Taliban fighter told Blaber that al-Qaeda treated the Taliban fighters "like we are dogs" (quoted in Blaber 2008: 246) with the Afghan rank and file strictly forbidden even to speak to the al-Qaeda mujahideen.

The valley was protected by a multilayered defense in depth. At the entrances to the valley, the insurgents maintained checkpoints which allowed them early warning of any ground-based intrusion into the Shahikot. As the official history of US Army SOF in Afghanistan relates, the valley was "classic guerrilla terrain – easily defendable, controlled access, numerous routes of escape, and near a sympathetic border" (Briscoe et al. 2003: 280).

The mujahideen had emplaced multiple 82mm and 120mm mortars covering the entrances to the valley, with the base plates often cemented into position to allow preregistered fire missions – another sign that whoever had developed the defenses knew what they were doing. A number of elderly but still lethal 76mm field guns and 122mm howitzers had also been emplaced in the valley with their arcs covering the entrances.

The air-defense network was similarly well sited. Weapons systems had been deployed to provide interlocking firing arcs against all likely avenues of approach by a heliborne force. These ranged from S-60 57mm antiaircraft guns to ZPU-1 14.5mm antiaircraft cannon. The eastern peaks were additionally defended by multiple DShK 12.7mm heavy machine guns on antiaircraft mounts, often in sandbagged positions with overhead cover. There was also at least one SA-7 Grail/Strela MANPADS available.

Thankfully there appears to have been no known use of American Stinger MANPADS that were a leftover from the Soviet–Afghan War. The battery packs fortunately had a relatively short "shelf life" that may explain their nonappearance. Whatever the reason, the lack of Stingers in enemy hands in the Shahikot was a blessing. Even one of the more advanced American MANPADS would have spelt disaster for the Chinooks of Task Force Rakkasan.

A door-gunner aboard a 160th SOAR MH-47E engages a target with his 7.62×51mm M134 minigun. Electrically powered, these guns were knocked out when RAZOR 01 lost its electrics during the crash landing on Takur Ghar. (DOD)

The static air defenses were very well placed on the so-called military crest of the mountains with the weapons systems oriented toward the valley, rather than on the tops of mountains where they would be more exposed to lethal fires from the USAF bombardment. Whoever had designed the defenses, most likely the elder Mansoor, he knew what he was doing and understood the likely avenues of attack.

The ridges were also peppered with caves, both natural and manmade, with some dating back to the 1980s. Major General Hagenbeck of the 10th Mountain explained in an interview with *Field Artillery* magazine in September/October 2002:

> The eastern ridge had more than one hundred caves dug in throughout the ridgeline. The enemy went from what appeared to be small fighting positions to the complex caves; the largest cave we found was about thirty meters deep in an inverted 'V' and then went right and left another thirty meters each. That cave was filled with weapons and ammunition caches. (McElroy 2002: 5)

Infiltration

On February 28, 2002, three AFO teams were covertly infiltrated into the valley. JULIET was an Army Delta element comprised of five operators including one signals-intelligence specialist from Grey Fox, the intelligence unit that conducts signals and electronic intelligence gathering for JSOC. The team entered from the north using Delta's specially modified ATVs and drove through snow, rain, and high winds using their night-vision devices to eventually reach an OP location on the east side of the valley. The second team was also an Army Delta element with an attached Grey Fox operator and was codenamed INDIA. This three-man team walked into the valley through the same incredibly fierce weather and climbed to establish their OP in the southwest of the valley in a location known as "The Fish Hook." The final team, MAKO 31, was from DEVGRU and was comprised of three SEALs, an Air Force Combat Controller, and, curiously, a Navy Explosive Ordnance Disposal (EOD) operator. It is unclear what

FEBRUARY 28, 2002

Operations begin in Shahikot Valley

support an EOD specialist could possibly provide to a covert surveillance team and his inclusion on the mission has never been explained. MAKO 31 also infiltrated on foot via the southern edge of the valley to set up their OP on a terrain feature known as "The Finger."

All three elements were tasked with covertly confirming enemy strengths and dispositions including anti-aircraft emplacements, ensuring the designated Rakkasan HLZs were clear of obstructions and providing terminal guidance for air support both prior to and during the insertion of the Rakkasans. The OP teams took advantage of the poor weather that kept the mujahideen in their caves and tents. The AFO teams wore a mix of Afghan and US clothing including camouflage "ghillie"-type suits known as Leafywear, were armed with both M4A1 carbines and the heavier-caliber SR-25 sniper rifle, and carried Schmidt-Cassegrain spotting 'scopes to enable them to plot enemy locations. Each team was also equipped with portable PRC-117F SATCOM radios linked to their Toshiba laptops to allow them to transmit grid locations and messages to the AFO Tactical Operations Center (TOC).

JULIET was in place by 04:45 whilst INDIA reached their OP at 10,500ft at 05:22, just beating the dawn. MAKO 31 had a very difficult infiltration route and ran out of darkness before they could reach their OP, stopping around 1,000m from their desired location. They would close the distance on the following night with day movement considered too risky with the large number of enemy evidently in the valley.

Also on February 28, the CIA flew a Mi-17 'Hip' helicopter in commercial markings down the valley to conduct an aerial reconnaissance. The 'Hip' carried a video camera that provided the Rakkasan leadership with some indication of the terrain they would be facing. AFO appears to have been opposed to the overflight on the basis that it may have spooked the enemy.

Whilst the AFO teams settled into their covert OPs, other special reconnaissance teams were also inserting into the valley. These teams were drawn principally from Task Force K-Bar and Task Force 64 and were tasked with establishing OPs which "had to be tenable, afford good reconnaissance, and cover the identified escape routes, or 'rat lines' into Pakistan" (quoted in Briscoe et al. 2003: 281) according to one of the planners. Some 25 teams from US and Coalition SOF including US Navy SEALs from Teams 2, 3, and 8, US Army Special Forces from the 3rd SF Group, and personnel from Canada's JTF-2, Australia's SASR, New Zealand's SAS Group, the German KSK, Norway's Jaegerkommando, the Dutch Korps Commandotroepen, and the Danish Army's Jaegerkorpset, were to be inserted on the outer edges of the valley to the east to cut off these potential escape routes. These SR

A slightly blurred image from the surveillance camera of MAKO 31, the SEAL team on "The Finger." It shows a mujahideen fighter, possibly a Chechen, checking on a 12.7mm DShK heavy machine gun on an antiaircraft tripod. This mujahideen along with his comrades was later killed by MAKO 31 and a follow-up AC-130 strike at about 04:00, two hours before the Rakkasans landed in the valley. (US Army)

teams largely remained uncompromised throughout the duration of *Anaconda* and provided vital intelligence which allowed air support to intercept enemy "squirters" and inhibit the ability of the enemy to reinforce positions (as an example, three NZSAS patrols remained in place without resupply for some ten days as did numerous other Coalition SOF teams).

First contact

The third AFO team, MAKO 31, moved into position during the predawn darkness of March 1. The team sent forward three SEALs to scout their proposed OP location before moving all of their equipment up and promptly discovered that the mujahideen had already established a fighting position exactly where their OP was to be located. Several enemy fighters appeared to be on the peak living in a large multiperson tent and had deployed a 12.7mm DShK heavy machine gun on a dedicated antiaircraft tripod. The DShK had excellent firing arcs over the southern end of the valley and could inflict serious damage on the Rakkasans' air assault if left in place.

The SEALs were surprised to see Caucasian-looking mujahideen moving around the location dressed in commercial cold-weather gear and what appeared to be Russian camouflage-pattern fatigues. MAKO 31 urgently informed AFO of their discovery and, not surprisingly, asked whether any British or Coalition Special Forces were operating at their location. Once they established there was no chance of fratricide and that the fighters were likely Chechens of the IMU, the SEALs developed a plan with AFO to attack and destroy the mujahideen position just before H-Hour, which was set for 06:30 on March 2.

JULIET also had a close call with a number of enemy fighters. On March 1, four or five mujahideen, braving the elements, trudged past JULIET's positions and appeared to spot the tracks of their ATVs. The mujahideen appeared confused by the tracks but eventually moved off without conducting any serious sweep of the area, leaving JULIET uncompromised.

The OP teams reported these ominous developments to AFO who passed

Another image from the surveillance camera of MAKO 31, showing "The Finger." Two foreign mujahideen are visible outside the tent the defenders of the peak slept in. These mujahideen were later killed by MAKO 31. (US Army)

them on to the Task Force Rakkasan leadership. The OP teams were also reporting large numbers of mujahideen moving about the valley and plotted numerous enemy positions on the ridges to the east and west. They also noted no evidence of any civilian occupation of the villages on the valley floor. All of the indications were that the civilian population had been forcibly displaced by the mujahideen and that the real threat was not on the valley floor but on the heights surrounding the Shahikot.

Seen through passive night vision, infantrymen from Task Force Rakkasan board their helicopters for the early-morning assault into the valley. (US Army)

As planned, several hours before the launch of Operation *Anaconda* (H-Hour or 06:30), MAKO 31 cautiously moved a three-man team forward toward the mujahideen position on "The Finger." The three DEVGRU snipers would engage the mujahideen at precisely 05:30 before withdrawing to allow an orbiting AC-130 Spectre to complete the job of destroying the DShK position with its heavier ordnance.

Luck was not on the team's side that morning. At approximately 04:00, a mujahideen left the tent and walked up the ridgeline, apparently looking for a spot to relieve himself. The SEALs tensed as the enemy fighter moved directly toward their position. The mujahideen suddenly spotted the SEALs, shouted a warning to his comrades, and ran back toward the tent. The team leader gave the order to engage and the three SEALs opened fire on the running mujahideen and the tent, inadvertently firing the first shots of Operation *Anaconda*.

Two of the three SEALs suffered stoppages with their M4A1 carbines, perhaps due to the climatic conditions, allowing five enemy to escape from the tent. Moments later, their carbines were firing again and three mujahideen were engaged and killed with aimed fire. The operators fired the remainder of their magazines into the tent and swiftly broke contact to allow the AC-130 to do its job.

GRIM 31, circling overhead, could see two further mujahideen moving around the back of the tent, attempting to flank the SEALs. One fired a burst from a Russian PKM general-purpose machine gun at the operators that fortunately missed. GRIM 31 cleared a "danger close" (bombs or other ordnance delivered close to friendly forces with the potential for wounding those friendlies) fire mission with MAKO 31, and as the SEALs took cover, delivered the first of several 105mm howitzer rounds down onto the peak. The first shell killed both remaining mujahideen with the follow-up rounds destroying the tent and the DShK position itself.

MAKO 31 swept through the mujahideen position to conduct a bomb damage assessment (BDA) and to recover any intelligence materials. The mujahideen were apparently very well equipped, with the PKM general-purpose machine gun, an RPG-7, a Dragunov SVD sniper rifle, and numerous AKs. In addition, the SEALs learnt that the DShK was likewise well supplied – some 2,000 rounds of ammunition sat in linked belts beside the gun that would have proved deadly to the lumbering Chinooks of Task Force Rakkasan.

Task Force Hammer

Zia Lodin's Task Force Hammer left Gardez as planned on the early morning of March 2. Soon, however, the plan began to unravel. Although there was nearly a full moon and good visibility, the Afghans were unfamiliar with driving at night and soon any pretense at light discipline was lost as the Afghans turned on their headlights. Numerous vehicles became bogged or broke down and the convoy suffered a rollover, which injured a dozen AMF.

Three ODA 372 soldiers with a handful of AMF broke off from the main column to establish an OP at the northern entrance to the valley to support Lodin's advance. The first tragedy of Operation *Anaconda* was about to occur. The pilot of GRIM 31, the orbiting AC-130 that had supported MAKO 31 minutes earlier, cleared fires against a small column of vehicles he could see on the ground and the weapons officer fired the AC-130's 40mm Bofors cannon into the group. ODA 372's Chief Warrant Officer Stanley Harriman was killed as were two AMF in the lead Ground Mobility Vehicle. Both of the other Special Forces soldiers were wounded as were seven AMF, some seriously. It was later established that GRIM 31's navigational systems were malfunctioning and that the location plotted for Harriman's convoy was not correct. Other SF soldiers quickly aborted any further fires from the AC-130 until they could establish what had occurred.

As the convoy finally moved off again, the first USAF bombs struck Tergul Ghar – seven Joint Direct Attack Munition (JDAM) smart bombs striking targets previously identified by the AFO and SASR teams. The ODAs and Lodin were stunned when the air strikes did not continue. They had been promised virtually a full hour of aerial bombardment prior to the attack and this had been a key leverage in convincing the Afghans to actually join the fight.

There is still confusion over exactly why the preparatory air strikes were aborted – several accounts mention an unspecified SOF element calling for the strikes to be halted as the ordnance was landing too close to their position, whilst others lay the blame at poor planning and coordination with the air component of *Anaconda*. Certainly the aircraft were in place at the right time – one B-1 bomber, one B-2 bomber, and a pair of F-15Es circled overhead, but only seven bombs were released.

Lodin's column eventually began to move forward again only to be struck by a heavy 82mm mortar barrage by the by-now fully awake and aware enemy. The Afghans moved forward once more until they finally halted before "The Whale." Lodin's own mortar crews were deployed and managed to fire several counterbattery fire missions against the emplaced enemy mortars.

The AMF were briefly supported by a pair of AH-64As who engaged enemy mortar crews on the western ridges of "The Whale." The attack helicopters were soon recalled to support Task Force Rakkasan as they prepared to air assault into the valley. This would be the only close air support (CAS) the AMF received that day. The attached ODAs attempted to rally the AMF but to no avail, and Task Force Hammer, frustrated by the lack of air support and with growing casualties from enemy mortars, finally withdrew to Gardez.

H-Hour

With the main effort halted and in disarray, the six CH-47D Chinook heavy-lift helicopters of Task Force Rakkasan thundered into the Shahikot Valley exactly on H-Hour at 06:30. The Rakkasans landed two rifle companies from each of the 2-187th and the 1-87th onto the valley floor. The 1-187th was also assigned to Task Force Rakkasan but was being held as a strategic reserve and Quick Reaction Force (QRF) and as such was not inserted with the initial Chinook lift. Overhead, five AH-64As (a sixth had been grounded with mechanical problems) from the 101st's Killer Spades flew air cover, watching for mujahideen weapons positions that could threaten the Chinooks.

Incredibly, the enemy defenders appeared to be surprised by the air assault and did not take the Chinooks under fire. This may perhaps be explained by the distraction of Task Force Hammer's advance and the fact that the various groups of enemies did not effectively communicate, negating a hasty response to the air assault operation into the valley. Such a response, resulting in even one downed helicopter, would have certainly been a disaster and changed the course of the battle.

As the soldiers raced down the helicopter ramps and quickly established perimeter security, the first shots rang out. Initially, the enemy small-arms fire was scattered and intermittent and the troops, many coming under fire for the first time, had difficulty locating the source of the incoming fire. Soon, the rate of fire increased as enemy gunners manned their heavy weapons and turned them toward the valley floor and the Rakkasans.

The two companies of the 2-187th landed in the northern end of the valley and began receiving effective enemy fire as they advanced but they managed to seize most of their closest BPs. The two companies of the 10th Mountain's 1-87th were landed at the southern end and experienced immediate and protracted resistance from the valley's defenders. The volume of fire pinned them down in a small depression that offered their only cover and which would become known as "Hell's Halfpipe."

As the men of Task Force Rakkasan attempted to suppress the enemy fire and secure their objectives, the AH-64As began engaging mujahideen positions on the ridges above. The Killer Spades encountered heavy resistance, with the enemy determined to bring down an Apache. The mujahideen used their DShKs and ZPU-1s along with bracketed

06:30, MARCH 3, 2002

Operation Anaconda begins

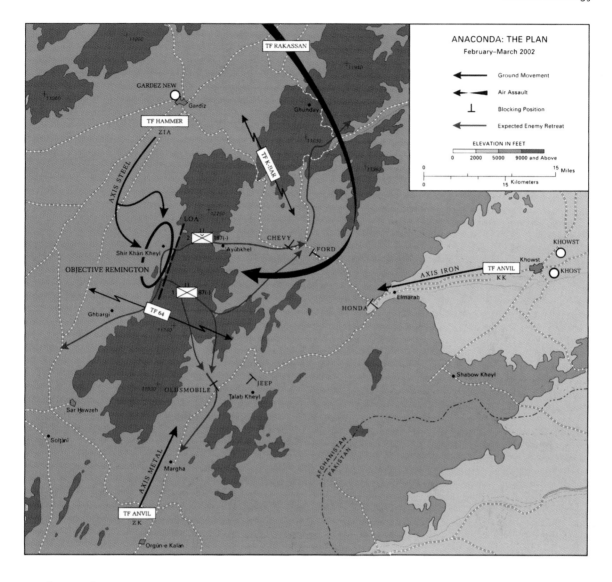

small-arms fire against the attack helicopters. The enemy also began firing their RPG rockets into the air, intending for the self-destruct mechanism that automatically detonates the warheads at 920m to catch the helicopters in lethal "flak bursts" of shrapnel. The Afghan mujahideen had long experience in using the RPG as a field-expedient antiaircraft weapon and these skills had been shared with their allies. The mujahideen in the Shahikot began to use another of these Soviet–Afghan War-era tactics – launching barrages of RPGs just ahead of the helicopters as the Apaches navigated through the valley.

Two Apaches were taken out of the fight early on the first day as they were peppered with RPG and machine-gun fire and forced to return to base. One AH-64A was hit by an RPG, which destroyed its left-side Hellfire mount, sending shrapnel through the airframe. The same Apache was also simultaneously engaged by a DShK, rounds from which actually penetrated the cockpit, narrowly missing the pilots. When the damaged helicopter was

A US military briefing map showing the projected locations of all elements before Task Force Hammer was left in disarray after the AC-130 friendly-fire incident and the lack of preparatory air strikes. Note the SOF teams deployed to assist in cutting off any withdrawing mujahideen. (US Army)

eventually landed, the crew counted more than 30 bullet holes in the fuselage in addition to the RPG damage.

On the ground, the infantrymen of Task Force Rakkasan were initially outgunned by the mujahideen. Their 5.56mm M4s and M249s did not have the range to effectively engage the valley's defenders. Nor did they have the penetrative power to punch through the enemy's prepared positions. Their few 7.62mm M240B general-purpose machine guns and the 40mm M203 launchers carried by every fire team were the only squad weapons systems that were proving effective in the difficult long-range environment they found themselves in.

The 2-187th brought with them no mortars in their initial Chinook lift. The 1-87th had brought in their organic 60mm infantry mortars and a single 120mm mortar that had only recently been added to the unit's Table of Organization and Equipment (TO&E). The mortars became the most effective infantry weapons of the battle with their ability to lob bombs into mujahideen fighting positions and suppress the enemy's heavy weapons. The enemy also quickly realized that the US mortars were the greatest threat and poured small-arms and mortar counterbattery fire against them. The sole 120mm mortar was soon fired dry after having expended the 35 bombs its crew brought in on the insertion.

No sooner would an enemy firing position be suppressed than another would pop up. The mujahideen used the network of caves and prepared positions to their advantage, moving between sites and hiding their mortars, machine guns, and recoilless rifles when air support was overhead. Major General Hagenbeck later explained in *Field Artillery* magazine:

> The al Qaeda soldiers would hear fixed wing aircraft overhead and quickly duck into the caves, protected from most air dropped munitions. So to get them, we had to put a JDAM inside the cave. But you only have so many of those precision munitions.
> To keep the enemy from ducking back into their caves, we used mortars and machine guns to kill them outright, when we could, or suppress them. We got a number of kills with close air support but they were primarily because our mortars and machine guns kept the al Qaeda from getting up and running back into the caves. (Quoted in McElroy 2002: 6)

Colonel Frank Wiercinski, commander of Task Force Rakkasan, was later quoted on the quality of the mujahideen in the Shahikot in a 2002 interview with noted columnist Austin Bay:

> They are tenacious. They wanted to go toe to toe with the US Army. They formed up there. They knew we could see them and come after them. They wanted to go face to face and say something. They were prepared. They had weapons systems they had been trained on: 82s, RPGs, small arms – AKs predominantly.
> And they are very good with 82 mm mortars. They're good with RPG tactics. I watched an Apache get hit with an RPG. I saw Apaches get hit with a lot of stuff and take it. I did not find them to be very good as marksmen, and they were not good at night. We owned the night. (Bay 2002)

Despite the heavy opposition, Task Force Rakkasan managed to secure their BPs to the north by the middle of the morning. After initially seizing a compound that had been very recently vacated by foreign mujahideen (leaving behind several SPG-9 recoilless rifles, RPG launchers, 82mm mortar bombs, and IED-making components), the men of the 2-187th began to take the fight to the enemy with units advancing up the difficult slopes to engage mujahideen positions.

The scheduled second lift of troops into the valley was postponed and eventually aborted due to increasingly poor weather and the tenacity of the enemy defenders – Task Force Rakkasan leadership were understandably concerned about a Chinook being lost to the significant air defenses in the valley. The men of the 10th Mountain at the southern HLZs were still pinned down, however. The 1st Platoon of Charlie Company of the 1-87th briefly secured one of their BPs before 82mm mortar fire wounded ten members of the platoon, forcing them to withdraw back into "Hell's Halfpipe."

Much of the fire directed at 1-87th was coming from the village of Marzak to the northwest of the depression they sheltered in. Hagenbeck explained: "Later on the first day and into the second day, when I declared two of the villages in the Shah-e-Kot Valley as targets, the aircraft leveled them – we had taken hostile fire from the villages and flown Predators over them to confirm their activities. The aircraft's precision munitions were most effective against those fixed targets" (quoted in McElroy 2002: 8).

Even with the fire from the village eliminated, mujahideen attempted to flank the 1-87th throughout the day. The battalion commander's tactical

A two-man sniper "pair" from the 101st Airborne search for targets in the Shahikot Valley on March 4, 2002. The spotter in the foreground is identifying insurgent positions with an M114 spotting 'scope for the sniper who is "on the gun" in the background, manning his 7.62×51mm M24 sniper rifle with mounted AN/PVS-10 Day/Night sight. The M24, with an effective range of 800m, was one of the few weapons initially deployed during *Anaconda* which could decisively engage the enemy at the extended ranges encountered in the valley. (Getty Images)

The Brigade Air Liaison Officer coordinates with MAKO 31's Combat Controller to guide in air strikes against targets in the Shahikot. This image was taken on "The Finger." (US Army)

HQ landed by UH-60 Blackhawk on a ridge below "The Finger" where MAKO 31 had earlier eliminated the mujahideen DShK position. The Blackhawk was fired upon both by RPGs and small-arms fire that narrowly missed the aircraft – if MAKO 31 had not destroyed the concealed DShK, doubtless the Blackhawk would have been shot down. The HQ element linked up with the AFO team before also being mortared. MAKO 31's attached Combat Controller joined forces with the battalion commander's air liaison officer to direct fast air onto the enemy mortar positions.

The other AFO teams continued to provide the best overview of enemy strengths and intentions from their mountaintop vantage points. Their only frustration was that Task Force Rakkasan had "priority of fires" over AFO and the other SOF SR teams surrounding the valley. This meant that if a Rakkasan Enlisted Terminal Attack Controller (ETAC) requested an air strike, his request would take precedence as they were classed as "troops in contact" whilst the special operators for the most part were not in direct contact with the enemy and thus their requests naturally took second place. The frustration was compounded as the AFO teams often had a far better read on the exact locations of enemy fire than the Rakkasans purely because of their location, and understanding and experience of the valley.

The Grey Fox operators of Task Force Orange attached to the OP teams also proved their worth, intercepting enemy communications and translating the intelligence to pass up the line. The signals-intelligence specialists managed to warn when the enemy was sending reinforcements or attempting to flank friendly forces on the valley floor. They even managed to triangulate the location of enemy spotters from their radio transmissions.

The Task Force Rakkasan leadership eventually decided that the second Chinook lift of troops would be inserted into the northern end of the valley to advance toward the southern end, clearing the eastern ridges as they went. The soldiers of the 1-87th, and their 26 wounded, would be extracted after dark. Task Force Hammer, and their SF advisors, had attempted another advance but again came under heavy and effective 82mm mortar fire. Receiving no air support as Rakkasan's plight, particularly in the southern end of the Shahikot, monopolized all available air assets, the Afghan fighters eventually withdrew once again back to Gardez, playing no further part in the fight.

As darkness finally fell on a long day of combat, the mighty AC-130s returned over the Shahikot and began to pummel enemy firing points. The men of the 1-87th marked targets by goading the enemy into firing. The return fire registered on the AC-130's sensors and was rapidly followed up with 105mm howitzer rounds. A HH-60G Pave Hawk was brought in to evacuate the most seriously wounded. The helicopter narrowly avoided an RPG fired at it and as it lifted off, a DShK opened fire on the departing HH-60G. The DShK position was noted by the orbiting AC-130 and as soon as the helicopter was clear of the airspace, the position was destroyed by a 105mm round.

Several hours later, the extraction Chinooks arrived and touched down near "Hell's Halfpipe," the AC-130s keeping a close eye on any enemy activity. The exhausted men piled aboard the pair of Chinooks and they lifted off without incident. The AC-130s had apparently cowed the enemy into submission and not a single round was fired at the helicopters as they flew up and away from the valley. The TAC HQ element near "The Finger," and overwatched by MAKO 31 who had returned to their OP, was also extracted by a Chinook in the same lift.

The next day, the strategic reserve component of Task Force Rakkasan, the 1-187th, was inserted into the northern end of the valley by Chinook supported by the Mortar Platoon of the 1-87th – this time with two 120mm and two 81mm mortar tubes. Linking up with the 2-187th, Task Force Rakkasan secured several BPs midway down the valley and took up static positions to allow close air support to pummel the enemy.

This image, taken from "The Finger" looking east, shows a string of Mark 82 500lb bombs being dropped from a B-52 upon targets near BP "Ginger." Takur Ghar can be seen to the far left of the bomb strikes. (US Army)

31

The air component had been significantly enhanced since the chaos of the first day. A flight of USAF A-10A Thunderbolt II ground-attack aircraft were deployed to Bagram and began near-constant sorties in support of the Rakkasans. Sixteen more Apaches from the 101st Aviation were deployed in support (replacing the one operational Apache left flying after the first day of the battle) as were five AH-1W Cobra gunships from the 13th Marine Expeditionary Unit. Major General Hagenbeck later commented on the close air support his men received during *Anaconda*:

> The most effective close air support asset we had was the Apache, hands down. The Apaches were extraordinary – they were lethal and survivable ... The detainees later said the Apaches were the most feared weapons on the battlefield – the helicopters were on top of them before they knew what was happening. The Apaches came as close to "one shot, one kill" as you can get.
>
> Our next most effective CAS assets were the A-10s in the daytime and AC-130s at night. They were great. We also had F-16s and F/A-18s and B-52s providing CAS. For the most part, they carried JDAMs and some dumb bombs. (Quoted in McElroy 2002: 7)

With the greatly expanded air support and reinforcements from the 1-187th, Task Force Rakkasan advanced down the Shahikot, clearing the ridges as well as the floor of the valley. The SOF OPs manned by the special operators of the SFO and Task Force K-Bar continued to severely hamper the ability of the enemy to reorganize or reinforce against the Rakkasans. However an urgent request by Task Force 11 leadership to insert further, probably unneeded, SOF teams into the fight, would soon end in disaster.

THE RAID

With the two Army and one Navy AFO OPs established and providing crucial intelligence and targeting for Task Force Rakkasan, at least one element of the operation was going to plan. This was soon to change. On March 2, Lieutenant Colonel Blaber, the AFO commander on the ground, received a surprising satellite telephone call from his boss, Brigadier General Trebon.

Essentially Trebon was ordering Blaber to hand over control of the AFO portion of the operation to the SEALs of Task Force Blue, who were moving teams in from Bagram to Gardez for this very purpose. Trebon couched the message in terms of AFO needing "to be out looking for the next battlefield" (quoted in Blaber 2008: 273) but was insistent that the SEALs be given the opportunity to join the fight and take over the operation from the Delta officer.

Blaber was, not surprisingly, stunned by this seemingly illogical request and responded that his teams were fine without resupply for at least another two days and that inserting new teams into the Shahikot immediately without any chance to understand the environment, acclimatize to the altitude, or gain precious advice from the AFO, CIA, and Special Forces was setting them up for failure.

Early the next morning on March 3, Blaber was awoken with the news that two SEAL force elements had arrived at the AFO safe house in Gardez. Blaber spoke with their newly arrived leader, Navy SEAL Lieutenant Commander Vic Hyder. Hyder repeated what Trebon had said and that he planned to insert the two SEAL elements, MAKO 21 and MAKO 30, as soon as possible. Blaber called Trebon in frustration and was met with a blunt response: "Put both of those SEAL teams into the fight tonight. That's an order" (quoted in Blaber 2008: 275).

Forced into a corner, Blaber and his AFO team had no option but to try to prepare the SEALs as best they could in the limited time available. Whilst AFO and their Special Forces colleagues attempted to bring the newly

Members of Task Force Rakkasan's command element including Colonel Frank Wiercinski take cover on "The Finger." Furthest from the camera is MAKO 31's Combat Controller firing a suppressed M4A1. Note the orange VS-17 identification panel next to him to mark their position to friendly air. (US Army)

arrived SEALs up to speed, the SEAL element leader, Hyder, surreptitiously set up an alternate radio link with Trebon and the Task Force 11 forward HQ in Bagram, bypassing the AFO team at Gardez.

The SEALs' initial plans were straightforward – the first team, MAKO 21, would link up with AFO team JULIET at the northern end of the valley, resupply them, and then establish an OP on the eastern ridge above Task Force Rakkasan's BPs. The second team, MAKO 30, would insert into an HLZ over 1km northeast of Takur Ghar before climbing to the peak to man their OP. Takur Ghar, being the highest mountain in the area, gave commanding, and strategic, views of the Shahikot and was an obvious site for an observation post. The two teams would insert that night, infiltrated into the AO by two MH-47E Chinooks of the 160th SOAR – RAZOR 03 and its wingman, RAZOR 04.

Initial infiltration of RAZOR 03

After delays from an inbound B-52 strike and a faulty MH-47E, which necessitated swapping airframes, RAZOR 03 and RAZOR 04 were finally in the air and heading toward their respective HLZs. The delays had taken precious time and, as dawn crept ever closer, MAKO 30 requested a 24-hour delay to allow an infiltration on the following night but Trebon said simply, "We need you to rethink that. We really need to get you in there tonight," according to author Malcolm Macpherson (Macpherson 2005: 14).

With the further delays, and Trebon's insistence on inserting the teams that night, the MAKO 30 team leader, Senior Chief Petty Officer Britt Slabinski (known as "Slab" and who later won the Navy Cross for his actions on Takur Ghar), felt he might have to look at an option Vic Hyder had discussed with him earlier – landing directly on the peak where they intended to establish their OP.

It seemed the only viable option if the team was to insert before daylight. Despite all of the warnings from the AFO team and the fact that he appears to have personally agreed with Blaber, MAKO 30's team leader had to follow the orders of both his direct boss and Trebon. He directed the Nightstalker crew to insert his team onto the summit of Takur Ghar.

NAIL 22, an orbiting AC-130, swept the peak with its sensors and declared the landing zone "cold" or uninhabited by enemy. The MAKO 30 team leader felt uneasy at the speed with which the sweep was conducted and wondered whether NAIL 22 had the right mountain. In any case, he soon dismissed his doubts and trusted to the AC-130's technology. As RAZOR 03 was inbound, NAIL 22 left the airspace to support an urgent "troops in contact" call from the Rakkasans in the valley, leaving the helicopter without the reassuring cover of the Spectre as it prepared to land.

The team was now landing on the mountaintop and not on an offset HLZ. This went against both AFO's stringent "no helicopter" rule and basic military tactics – landing on the site of the intended OP invited trouble. In HVT raids, the helicopters would often land directly "on the X" as speed was the key consideration in killing or capturing the HVT before he could escape or mount a defense. In special reconnaissance, it simply meant warning the enemy that a friendly force had landed in the area and all but pinpointed the location of the OP.

Landing at an offset HLZ and walking in gave the team a much better chance of remaining undetected. With the evident time pressures, and the additional pressure placed upon him from the geographically remote Task Force 11 leadership, Slab was left with little to no choice but to go against these cardinal rules and land his team on the peak.

MAKO 30

With the well-known secrecy of JSOC, it is difficult to know exactly how the MAKO 30 element were armed and equipped; however, a reasonably accurate picture can be developed from various sources. The team went in with its primary purpose being surveillance but with enough firepower to hopefully fight their way out of any trouble.

It appears the team member known only as "Brett" carried an M60E4, otherwise known as the Mk 43 Mod 0, a belt-fed 7.62×52mm general-purpose machine gun that was the latest iteration of the famous Vietnam-era M60. The Mk 43 Mod 0 features a forward handgrip and is lightened from its predecessor specifically to allow firing from the shoulder on the move. Mk 43s used by DEVGRU often featured a combat optic, the Trijicon Advanced Combat Optical Gunsight (ACOG), mounted upon the receiver. The ACOG provides a four-power magnified image which assists with both accuracy and target discrimination. This machine gun was the heaviest weapon available to MAKO 30 on the mountaintop.

Petty Officer First Class Neil Roberts carried a 5.56×45mm Squad Automatic Weapon (SAW) that served as the light machine gun for SEAL Teams. It is likely the SAW deployed by Roberts was either an early Mk 46 Mod 0 or the Minimi SPW (Special Purpose Weapon) variant. Both are modified versions of the US military's standard M249 SAW with shortened barrels, lighter weight, and added Picatinny rails for the mounting of accessories such as optics, weapon lights, and foregrips. Both the SPW and the Mk 46 were developed specifically for USSOCOM and JSOC units.

There is some conjecture about the exact armament of the other SEALs in the element but it appears that the team leader, "Slab," and two other SEALs – "Randy" and "Kyle" – carried Stoner SR-25 7.62×51mm sniper rifles featuring bipods, sound suppressors, and Leupold optical 'scopes. They also mounted AN/PEQ-2 infrared illuminators, used to mark targets

ARMS AND EQUIPMENT

In the foreground is shown a SEAL from the DEVGRU AFO teams dressed and equipped in a similar manner to the members of MAKO 30 on Takur Ghar. This representative SEAL is armed with a 7.62×51mm Knight's Armament Corporation SR-25 sniper rifle with a Leupold Vari-X telescopic 'scope and folded Harris bipod. The SR-25 also features a Knight's Armament suppressor that reduces both the report and muzzle flash of the weapon. As a backup to the SR-25, he also carries a 9×19mm SIG Sauer P226 semiautomatic pistol in a drop holster on his right thigh. Below is the 7.62×51mm Mk 43 Mod 0 machine gun.

He wears US Army issue Gore Tex jacket and trousers in three-color desert-pattern camouflage. His boots are privately purchased commercial hiking boots that are worn in preference to military boots by many in SOF. His body armor is an early example from Eagle Industries of their CIRAS (Combat Integrated Releasable Armor System), a vest that became popular amongst Tier One units. His magazine pouches are fitted directly to the CIRAS as is a pouch for his MBITR intrasquad radio.

The SEAL's helmet is a Pro-Tec skateboard/snowboard helmet. The helmet is constructed from plastic and offers no ballistic protection although it does protect the user from knocks and scrapes whilst climbing or operating in tight confines. Upon the helmet is mounted an infrared strobe to allow identification of friendly personnel, particularly from the air, using night-vision goggles. The helmet also features an American flag attached by Velcro and a mounting bracket for night-vision goggles. This SEAL wears Scott brand goggles to protect his eyes from the snow and wind of the mountains.

Behind the SEAL is a representative figure of a Ranger equipped in the type of equipment that the Rangers of the QRF carried into battle. This Ranger's primary weapon is the 5.56×45mm Colt M4A1 carbine mounting a vertical foregrip, an AN/PEQ-2 infrared illuminator, and M68 Aimpoint 'red dot' sight. He also carries a pistol as a back-up weapon, in this case a standard Army issue 9×19mm Beretta M9 in an issue drop holster.

The Ranger also wears Gore Tex desert-pattern jacket and trousers and Nomex aviator gloves. He wears a Ranger issue Rack load-bearing system carrying his ammunition and grenades over a SPEAR body armor vest in woodland camouflage pattern. He also carries an MBITR radio with Peltor headset, which allows the use of the radio along with offering noise reduction of loud sounds such as gunshots or explosions.

Finally, the Ranger wears a MICH ballistic helmet with night-vision mounting bracket (with a Velcro attachment on the crown with an infrared 'glint' patch attached which is visible only through night vision), issue kneepads in woodland pattern, and a pair of commercially purchased Merrell hiking boots.

and to provide an infrared light source that is only visible through night-vision devices.

The SR-25 was a popular choice in Afghanistan due to its longer range and thanks to its heavier 7.62mm caliber, ruggedness, and semiautomatic capability. This final element made it a strong contender against traditional bolt-action sniper rifles as it allowed for either fast follow-up shots or to be used *in extremis* in a close-quarter engagement as an assault rifle. The Delta operators within AFO and the Australian SASR teams deployed into the valley also favored the SR-25 for similar reasons.

The Air Force Combat Controller, Technical Sergeant John A. "Chappy" Chapman, carried a camouflage-painted 5.56×45mm M4A1 SOPMOD carbine, equipped with a Knight's Armament suppressor, AN/PEQ-2 infrared illuminator, and an Aimpoint M68 combat optic. Another MAKO 30 SEAL, known as "Turbo," also carried an M4A1, most likely with a 40mm M203 grenade launcher mounted under the barrel. The M203 can fire a range of grenade types including high explosive and chemical smoke out to ranges of several hundred meters.

All of the MAKO SEALs carried sidearms – the SEALs preferred the 9×19mm SIG Sauer P226. They carried both fragmentation and smoke grenades. It also appears, from at least one account, that several of the SEALs, including their team leader, carried stand-alone 40mm grenade launchers. These would most likely have been the Vietnam-era M79 that is still used by some US Army Special Forces and SEALs, as it is regarded as being both more accurate and having a greater range than the newer M203 system. It is known that JSOC units such as DEVGRU use a custom-made cut-down M79 grenade launcher with much of the stock and barrel cut away and fitted with a holographic weapon sight developed by unit armourers. This cut-down M79 is known as the 'pirate gun' within DEVGRU due to its resemblance to a flintlock pistol.

A final member of the initial team, not mentioned in most accounts, was an operator from JSOC's secretive Grey Fox. It is unknown how this operator, nicknamed "Thor," was armed, but an M4A1 or M4A1/M203 combination is a likely bet. He also carried portable signals intelligence (SIGINT) equipment that allowed him to monitor and/or electronically jam enemy communications.

Like all of the AFO teams, MAKO 30 also carried perhaps the most important equipment to successfully prosecute their special reconnaissance mission – a Nikon Coolpix digital camera equipped with an eight-power magnification lens and a "ruggedized" (toughened) Toshiba Libretto laptop which could be used to transmit images via the SATCOM radio carried by Chapman back to AFO and Task Force 11 headquarters.

The team all wore Gore Tex Extreme Cold Weather BDUs in three-color desert pattern and used a mixture of commercially purchased chest rigs and load carriers. Some also used gaiters to counter the heavy snow in the mountains surrounding the Shahikot. Their Pro-Tec-style helmets were non-ballistic (in that they provided no protection against bullets or shrapnel fragment) and were intended as protection against falls during the arduous climb they originally planned for.

RAZOR 03

At just before 02:50, the MH-47E flared in to land on the peak. As he came closer to the snow-covered ground, one of the 160th SOAR pilots spotted a sandbagged 12.7mm DShK heavy machine-gun position farther up the slope. It was unmanned. As the pilot informed his crew and the SEALs, he pondered whether it could have been a long-forgotten relic of the Soviet–Afghan War.

Moments later, as the Chinook settled into a landing, a crew chief shouted that he could see a tethered donkey farther up the slope in the treeline. Another crewmember called that he could see goat carcasses hanging in nearby trees. Finally a rear gunner spotted an individual raise his head from behind the boulders on the slope and quickly duck back down again. It was now very questionable whether the peak was as uninhabited as NAIL 22's sensors had earlier indicated.

Slab made the command decision that the team would insert and as he prepared to order his team off the helicopter, an RPG came screaming past the cockpit. Moments later, machine-gun fire erupted from the treeline and rounds began to punch through the thin, unarmored sides of the Chinook. A second RPG flew toward them and this time hit home, striking just behind the cockpit and starting an internal fire in the cabin.

c.02:50,
MARCH 4

RAZOR 03 Chinook fired upon; SEAL Neil Roberts lost

Some of the damage sustained by RAZOR 03 that attempted to insert MAKO 30 onto Takur Ghar. In the close-up, the fuel bladder has sustained an RPG strike and the airframe has been hit numerous times by small arms of varying calibers. (USASOC)

Yet another RPG struck seconds after first hit, exploding into the Chinook's right-side radar pod. This hit also blew out all AC electrical power to the aircraft, leaving many of the navigation systems out of action and the electrically powered miniguns useless (this incident led to 160th SOAR developing a battery-powered backup system for the miniguns which is in use today).

Another RPG impacted outside the aircraft, sending razor-sharp fragments through the Chinook. A further RPG struck a moment later, hitting the right-side turbine. They were also taking heavy automatic-weapons fire from at least three distinct firing points, including a Russian-made PKM general-purpose machine gun. Thankfully, the helicopter had set down in a slight depression, shielding it from the heavy DShK the pilots had seen. The pilot made the call to save his passengers and the aircraft by getting out of the ambush as quickly as possible and yanked the controls to bring the Chinook back into the air.

As he did so, the Chinook swerving violently to present a more difficult target to the enemy, the SEAL closest to the ramp fell and slid towards the edge. One of the SOAR crew chiefs, wearing a restraining tether, managed to grab hold of the SEAL's pack but lost his grip as the helicopter again swerved to avoid ground fire. The SEAL disappeared over the edge of the ramp and was lost to the night.

Roberts

At approximately 02:50, Petty Officer First Class Neil Christopher "Fifi" Roberts, a ten-year veteran of the SEALs, fell some 10ft from the MH-47E's open ramp and into the knee-deep snow covering the peak of Takur Ghar. He carried only his SAW, his SIG Sauer pistol and several grenades. Realizing his predicament, Roberts quickly activated the infrared strobe that all Task Force 11 members carried to mark their positions at night for friendly forces, particularly for air cover such as the lumbering but deadly AC-130H Spectre.

Tragically, and perhaps because of the accelerated timeline forced upon MAKO 30 by Task Force 11 headquarters, the closest AC-130, GRIM 32, did not have the team's radio frequencies loaded. According to Sean Naylor, all other AFO elements routinely loaded the frequency for the ever-present AWACS (Airborne Warning And Control System) known as BOSSMAN in case of an *in extremis* close air support request had to be relayed via the AWACS. MAKO 30 had not done this.

Roberts' Multi-Band Intra-Team Radio (MBITR) radio, only designed for line-of-sight communications, was effectively useless. The only other radio, a powerful SATCOM set, was carried by Chapman, the Special Tactics airman back on the stricken RAZOR 03. Any account of Roberts' next actions are, at best, assumptions based on accounts of what was allegedly seen by the AC-130 crew through their optics. An RQ-1 Predator UAV did not arrive on station until some 90 minutes after Roberts fell and gives no further clues.

From these accounts and forensic evidence later recovered from the mountain, it appears Roberts engaged the mujahideen fighters from the IMU on the peak and became involved in a heavy firefight. His night-vision goggles and PEQ-2 infrared illuminator mounted on his SAW would have given him some small advantage over his opponents but he was outnumbered and surrounded. His SAW became disabled at some point by enemy fire and Roberts was struck in the upper right thigh by an enemy round, dropping him into the snow. His SIG Sauer pistol was later recovered unfired and still in its holster so it is assumed that blood loss finally took its inevitable toll on the SEAL and he lapsed into unconsciousness.

Petty Officer First Class Neil Roberts, killed on top of Takur Ghar on March 4. (US Navy)

Again, from observers who have watched the footage from GRIM 32's cameras, it appears that Roberts was quickly surrounded by mujahideen who dragged the fallen SEAL farther up the peak to a point near the bunker. Major General Hagenbeck, commander of Task Force Rakkasan, reported in a 2002 interview: "The image was fuzzy, but we believe it showed three al-Qaeda had captured Roberts and were taking him away around to the south side of [blocking position] Ginger and disappearing into a tree line. That was 15 to 20 minutes before the first rescue team arrived" (quoted in Bradley 2002).

It was at 04:27 that Roberts was executed by a single AK round to the head by one of the Uzbeks, a fact supported by the gunshot hole found in Roberts' Pro-Tec helmet (Staff Sergeant Canon, part of the Ranger QRF, reported that he thought Roberts' throat had been hacked open but this damage may have been caused posthumously by close air support strikes in the area around his body).

The Uzbeks pilfered a spare set of Gore Tex BDUs in three-color desert pattern, his woolen watch cap and various other items from his vest and rucksack. Accounts suggest they even passed around the infrared strobe (it is not known whether it was helmet-mounted or a handheld unit) for some time before turning it off and retreating to their bunkers.

The final moments of Roberts' life were witnessed (at least to some degree) by the crew of GRIM 32 who were frustratingly forced to hold their fire in the chaos of conflicting orders reaching them from Task Force 11 headquarters in Masirah, the AFO TOC at Gardez, and the newly established Task Force Blue TOC at Bagram. Blaber and his deputy, Major "Jimmy," also a respected Delta officer, had the best chance of managing the situation on the mountaintop but were drowned out by contradictory and ill-informed orders from Task Force 11 who were some 1,600km from the battlespace.

The AFO commander ordered GRIM 32 to fire into the group on the peak and hopefully disperse them to the point that it would become clear who was Roberts either from his strobe or from the fact that he would likely be trying to escape his pursuers. It was a hasty plan but it was Roberts' best chance at survival. Unfortunately that plan was never enacted in a jumble of mixed messages that left the AC-130 crew no closer to understanding what was happening on the mountain.

04:27, MARCH 4

Roberts shot by mujahideen

The rescue attempt

RAZOR 03 managed to clear the peak under heavy ground fire. The pilots kept the stricken Chinook aloft for a bare 7km from Takur Ghar until they were forced to make a hard landing in a clearing some 2,000ft lower than the mountain, shortly before 03:00. The SEALs immediately provided 360-degree security around the airframe whilst Chapman got onto the communications net and managed to divert another AC-130, callsign GRIM 33, to scan their surroundings for enemy whilst tasking GRIM 32 to return to the peak in an attempt to ascertain Roberts' status.

GRIM 33, and a circling P-3 Orion surveillance aircraft, picked up thermal heat signatures from a large group of individuals near the crashlanded Chinook although there is still some question whether these were, in fact, friendly-force elements from the Rakkasans. The AC-130 stayed on station to protect RAZOR 03 whilst a second MH-47E was flown up from Gardez. Slab, the MAKO team leader, wanted the second MH-47E to pick them up and fly them directly to the peak to try to rescue Roberts.

However, he was told in no uncertain terms that they would first return to Gardez, drop off the Grey Fox operator and the crew of RAZOR 03 along with much of the now not-needed gear including Chapman's SATCOM radio set, surveillance spotting 'scopes, spare cold weather gear, cameras, and their backpacks. Their objective had rapidly changed – MAKO 30 were now on a direct-action recovery mission, not special reconnaissance, and they needed ammunition more than cameras.

When the replacement helicopter, callsign RAZOR 04, arrived at 03:45, MAKO 30 and the crew of RAZOR 03 boarded and the helo flew them all back to Gardez against the continual strong objections of the SEALs. They unloaded the 160th personnel, the Grey Fox operator, and their extra equipment quickly and lifted off at 04:45 to return to Takur Ghar.

The helicopter was unfortunately now critically low on fuel and with no time to refuel (there were no refueling stations at Gardez at that time), the crew of RAZOR 04 would only have one chance to insert the SEALs and no opportunity to look for a safer, offset HLZ. It was going to have to be the peak, a known "cherry" HLZ ("cherry" denotes a "hot" or contested HLZ whilst "ice" denotes a safe HLZ with no obvious enemy presence).

The SEALs made contact with GRIM 32, the AC-130 still on station over the mountain, and requested pre-assault fires from the gunship one minute prior to touchdown. The crew of GRIM 32 (piloted by the same pilot who had flown GRIM 31 two days earlier when it was involved in the friendly-fire incident that killed Special Forces Chief Warrant Officer Stanley Harriman and several AMF from Task Force Hammer) would not agree the request as they could not clearly identify Roberts and were understandably worried their fires might injure or kill him. The crew was also still confused about the exact situation on the ground as numerous headquarters elements issued conflicting orders.

GRIM 32, trying to assist RAZOR 04 in some way, identified a safer offset HLZ for the insertion; however, communications had by this stage broken down between the AC-130 and the inbound MH-47E. Officially,

04:45, MARCH 4

RAZOR 04 and MAKO 30 take off to return to Takur Ghar

there were technical issues with the satellite-communications sets although some accounts allege that RAZOR 04 simply stopped talking to the gunship after preparatory fires were denied. The AC-130 wrongly assumed that RAZOR 04 was coming in on the offset HLZ they had identified and were shocked when moments later the Chinook swung in to land directly on the peak at 04:55. Some 30 minutes after Roberts had been excuted, his teammates had returned to attempt to rescue him.

Back on the peak

As RAZOR 04 flared in to land, the mujahideen defenders of Takur Ghar could not believe their luck when yet another American helicopter was landing on the mountain peak. They quickly manned their positions and the heavy 12.7mm DShK opened fire on the Chinook. Soon, small-arms and PKM fire joined in with the heavy machine gun. One of the door-gunners managed to fire off only a few rounds in response before his minigun suffered a stoppage. RAZOR 04, remarkably, landed relatively in one piece. With the ramp down, the SEALs and Chapman charged off into the knee-deep snow in search of their comrade.

At first, the enemy didn't spot the SEALs in the early-morning darkness and concentrated their fire at RAZOR 04. Finally the helicopter lifted off and escaped the lethal barrage. MAKO 30 had split up into two-man buddy pairs to conduct bounding movement and they were making good ground until the enemy finally spotted them. Chapman had advanced ahead of Slab and stumbled across an enemy bunker on the peak under the trees.

He quickly shot its three occupants with his suppressed M4A1 carbine before Slab caught up with him, undoubtedly saving the rest of the team from what would certainly have been devastating fire as they advanced up the peak. Suddenly, whilst both men crouched at the bunker, a PKM

An armed RQ-1 Predator of the type which provided vital close air support to the Rangers. This Predator carries two AGM-114 Hellfire II guided antitank missiles. Recent versions now have the capability to carry a GBU-38 500lb JDAM. (DOD)

TAKUR GHAR: The Rangers' battle on the peak

MARCH 4, 2002

US MILITARY PERSONNEL
LOCATIONS, c.06:21 1-12

1 Staff Sergeant Gabe Brown USAF

2 Technical Sergeant John A. Chapman USAF (KIA)

3 Staff Sergeant Ray DePouli

4 Private First Class David Gilliam

5 Specialist Anthony Miceli

6 Petty Officer First Class Neil Roberts USN (KIA)

7 Captain Nate Self

8 Chief Warrant Officer Class 5 Don Tabron

9 Specialist Aaron Totten-Lancaster

10 Staff Sergeant Kevin Vance USAF

11 Sergeant Joshua Walker

12 Sergeant Brian Wilson

MUJAHIDEEN TENT

DShK POSITION (BELOW RIDGE)

BUNKER

TRENCH

BUNKER

BUNKER

C E

H

D

9
11
7
10
3
4

6
2

H

EVENTS

A 06:10: RAZOR 01 undertakes forced landing

B 07:20–07:50: F-15E sortie with 20mm cannon

C 08:01–08:26: F-16CG sortie with 20mm cannon

D 08:07: Chalk 1 launches first ground assault; unsuccessful

E 08:45–09:34: F-15E and F-16CG sorties with 500lb bombs

F 09:44: MQ-1 Predator attack with Hellfire II missiles

G 10:20: Chalk 2 find Roberts' gear; link up with Chalk 2

H 11:02: Chalk 1 and Chalk 2 launch second ground assault; successful

I 11:45: Mujahideen counterattack; unsuccessful

Captain Nate Self pictured near the Tarnak Farms complex prior to the QRF mission on March 4, 2002. (US Army)

Captain Nate Self pictured near the Tarnak Farms complex prior to the QRF mission on March 4, 2002. (US Army)

general-purpose machine-gun crew, sited in a second bunker farther back behind the first, opened fire on them. Two of the other SEALs attempted to outflank the second bunker only to be driven to cover by the huge weight of fire.

The team leader fired two 40mm grenades at the second bunker, both without any appreciable effect. Chapman, crouching next to Slab, was hit by an enemy round from the bunker and fell forward into the snow. Slab had to take out the bunker before he could treat Chapman so he fired three more 40mm grenades at the bunker. The target was just inside the minimum safety distance for the 40mm grenades and most didn't explode. Frustrated, Slab fired off a volley of grenades at the enemy off to his left who were firing at the other SEALs before finally launching his last two grenades toward the DShK position. With his ammunition expended, he dropped the launcher to the ground and shouldered his SR-25.

Kyle and Brett were pinned down behind a rocky outcrop to the left of Slab, taking fire from both the DShK position and the second bunker. Slab quickly coordinated with them and Brett bravely stood up, firing his M60E4 from the shoulder down into the bunker. One of the other SEALs, presumably Kyle, threw two hand grenades at the bunker, temporarily suppressing the mujahideen fire.

Slab and Kyle moved out of cover to close-assault the bunker but as they broke cover, a Soviet fragmentation grenade was lobbed toward them. The grenade detonated in front of the rock they were using for cover, wounding Brett in the foot. Moments later, an IMU fighter armed with an AK-47 boldly stepped from the bunker and shot the already wounded Brett twice in the legs.

Slab looked across at Chapman and saw no sign of life. Earlier he could see Chapman's IP laser moving up and down with his labored breathing. Now he could see no such sign. He crawled over Chapman's motionless legs but did not try to speak to him as Slab didn't want to give away his position with the enemy in such close proximity.

With Brett seriously wounded, Kyle lightly wounded and Chapman apparently dead, Slab had no choice but to give the order to break contact with the enemy and withdraw from the peak. He lobbed a chemical smoke grenade to cover their retreat as the SEALs withdrew using bounding movement, covering each other as they ran towards a ledge on the eastern side of the peak. As they ran, Turbo was hit, nearly severing one of his feet at the ankle. Randy grabbed him and moved him out onto the ledge into cover.

After a 22-minute firefight, MAKO 30, with one dead, two seriously wounded and one lightly wounded, was combat ineffective.

QRF

Upon reaching cover on the narrow ledge to the east of the peak, the team leader immediately contacted the orbiting AC-130, GRIM 32, via his MBITR line-of-sight team radio to request both immediate fire support and to relay his request for the Task Force 11 QRF to be launched from Bagram. The AC-130 asked Slab to turn on his IR strobe to identify himself and his men before beginning to fire upon the bunkers and trees with the heaviest weapon system the gunship carried, the 105mm howitzer.

A mujahideen 82mm mortar crew then began firing onto the peak, seemingly indiscriminately and without regard to the chance of hitting their own fighters, forcing the SEALs to scramble farther down the side of the mountain to a shelf that sheltered them from the bombs. As the first 105mm rounds from the AC-130 thundered into the enemy positions on Takur Ghar, the call for the QRF reached Bagram.

35 Rangers from the 1st Platoon, Alpha Company, 1st Battalion of the 75th Ranger Regiment led by Captain Nate Self had been assigned the duty of QRF for all Task Force 11 operations. Only half of the platoon was available that day as the remainder was conducting live-fire training at Tarnak Farms, a former home to none other than bin Laden.

The QRF Rangers were on "strip alert" at Bagram waiting for the call to assist troops in contact or downed aviators. The call from GRIM 32 was eventually channeled to the Task Force 11 TOC at Bagram and Self and his men were assigned the mission. The information provided by the TOC to Self was confused and contradictory – the initial call was for the downed Chinook, RAZOR 03, but that soon changed with reports of an operator falling from a helicopter. The QRF were not even informed of the existence of MAKO 30 until they were airborne.

Self had an amalgamated eight-man Ranger chalk comprised of a squad leader, one three-man fire team and one two-man fire team, and a two-man machine-gun team. Staff Sergeant Ray DePouli led the Ranger element, known as Chalk 1, that included Sergeant Joshua Walker, Sergeant Bradley Crose, grenadier Private First Class Matt Commons, SAW gunners Specialist Aaron Totten-Lancaster and Specialist Anthony Miceli, and the machine-gun team of Specialist Marc Anderson and his assistant gunner, Private First Class David Gilliam.

ETAC Staff Sergeant Kevin Vance USAF, Captain Self's principal air controller on Takur Ghar. He carries a modified M4A1 carbine with M68 Aimpoint, AN/PEQ-2, and Surefire light. (US Air Force)

The majority of the Rangers carried M4A1 carbines with mounted PEQ-2 infrared markers, Surefire tactical lights, and M68 Aimpoint "red dot" optics. Commons had the only 40mm M203 grenade launcher amongst the team mounted under the barrel of his carbine. Each Ranger carried between ten and 15 30-round magazines of ammunition for their M4A1s and additional ammunition for the SAWs and M240B. Totten-Lancaster and Miceli carried the squad support weapons – the 5.56mm M249 SAWs – while the hulking Anderson manned the big 7.62mm M240B.

Also directly under Self's command was his assigned Air Force ETAC, Staff Sergeant Kevin Vance, who would serve as his link to the vital close air support. Attached to the Rangers for the mission were three members of the Air Force's Special Tactics Squadrons (STS) – two Pararescue Jumpers known as PJs (rescue specialists highly trained in combat medicine), Technical Sergeant Keary Miller and Senior Airman Jason Cunningham, plus a Combat Controller, Staff Sergeant Gabe Brown, who carried out a similar role to Vance, the attached ETAC.

Staff Sergeant Arin Canon commanded the second Ranger chalk, Chalk 2, on board RAZOR 02. Canon led ten Rangers comprising Staff Sergeant Harper Wilmoth, a two-man fire team and a three-man fire team each carrying two M249 SAWs and two M203 launchers in addition to their M4A1 carbines, a two-man machine-gun team carrying the M240B, and a combat medic. Both Ranger chalks and the Nightstalker crews were still receiving contradictory information that would only increase once they were in the air.

Just after 05:00, RAZOR 01, carrying Self's Chalk 1, lifted off from Bagram with RAZOR 02 following minutes later. At first, the helicopters were directed to the forward staging area at Gardez where they were told that they would be briefed on a plan, but that directive soon changed mid-flight when they were ordered to fly finally toward the Shahikot.

During the flight, Self received further information that his team was to land and extract a "SEAL sniper team" that was in contact with the enemy.

At that point, the information the QRF was receiving indicated, falsely as it turned out, that Roberts had already linked up with the MAKO 30 element. The SATCOM radios on board the 160th SOAR Chinooks were also malfunctioning and meant that the aircrews had limited contact with their headquarters element who were issuing the orders and updates.

Above the mountain, GRIM 32 continued to provide supporting fires to MAKO 30 as the sun slowly rose. AC-130s were prohibited from flying in daylight since the 1991 shootdown of an AC-130 during the battle of Khafji on the Kuwaiti border. The AFO commander, Blaber, repeatedly urged the AC-130 to stay on station until the QRF arrived, only minutes away. The MAKO 30 team leader also pleaded with the aircrew to continue their vigil until other aircraft could be on-station overhead.

GRIM 32 were in an unenviable position, ignoring repeated calls for them to return to base as they tried to stay over the battlespace for as long as possible. The Spectre had also had two suspected MANPADS SAMs fired at them as the enemy began to be able to make out the aircraft's shape in the increasing light. GRIM 32 finally had to turn for home at 06:05 as the fuel status became critical.

A pair of Air Force F-15Es were inbound and being vectored to the airspace to continue to provide vital close air support. As the AC-130 pulled away for its flight home, the aircrew passed the coordinates of the offset HLZ they had identified to an orbiting AWACS and reiterated the warning about landing on the peak: "Whatever you do, don't send them [the QRF] back to this same LZ. It is absolutely hot!" (Naylor 2005: 338).

The SEALs of MAKO 30 had moved on from their initial refuge and were now approximately 1km down the face of the mountain, shielded away from enemy fire from the peak. With the communications chaos, it was still believed by Task Force 11 headquarters that they were in direct contact with the enemy on the HLZ. No mention of the loss of Chapman or any clarification that Roberts was or was not still missing was passed on to the Rangers. As far as Captain Self's team were aware, they were still inserting on a "cherry" HLZ to extract the SEALs. Self informed his men via a light board in the back of RAZOR 01 – "SEAL snipers in contact w/enemy vic[inity of] LZ. Hot extraction on a hot LZ. Watch your fires" (Self 2008: 148).

This was not the only incorrect information to be given to RAZOR 01 and Ranger Chalk 1. The orbiting Navy P-3 Orion, codenamed TOOLBOX, acting as an airborne relay station between the MH-47Es somehow managed to give the Chinooks the wrong coordinates for the HLZ. Instead of the planned offset HLZ some 800m from the crest, the P-3 appears to have passed the Chinook the coordinates for the peak itself.

The 160th SOAR command on Masirah Island realized the error and desperately tried to contact the Chinooks or the P-3 to try and avert disaster but with the choppy radio reception, their message to abort came too late. RAZOR 02 carrying Canon's Chalk 2 was placed in a holding pattern due to the small size of the HLZ. Shortly before 06:10, RAZOR 01 and Self's Rangers circled in to the peak of Takur Ghar with the sun just beginning to rise over the mountains to the east.

c.05:00, MARCH 4

With five casualties, MAKO 30 is combat ineffective

c.05:17, MARCH 4

QRF Rangers take off in RAZOR 01 and 02

Ambush

The crew of the Chinook could see no sign of the SEAL team as they neared the HLZ but saw much evidence of the recent battle – craters from the 40mm and 105mm rounds from GRIM 32, footprints in the snow and, most worryingly, what appeared to be the small-arms muzzle flashes from around the crest of the mountain where the enemy bunkers and gun positions lay.

As they flared in, they began receiving effective fire as the enemy small-arms fire began to strike the MH-47E. Both the pilot and co-pilot were struck by rounds but held the aircraft steady (the pilot was hit ten times with all but one striking his body armor and helmet). Both right-side door-gunners opened fire in response (MH-47Es feature a forward and rear door-gunner on both sides of the aircraft – the forward gunner mans an M134 minigun whilst the rear gunner mans the elderly but still effective M60D). Moments later, an RPG-7 rocket exploded into the right-side turbine and the Chinook lost power and dropped the final 15ft at a speed of 500ft per minute to the snow-covered slope.

The Chinook, now without AC electrical power and with its electrically powered miniguns hanging useless in their mounts, managed a hard landing onto a twenty-degree slope facing upward toward the enemy bunkers and the large rocks at the top of the rise. The only saving grace was that it was too far down the slope for the enemy's 12.7mm DShK to engage it. Mujahideen fighters, now fully alert, again scrambled from their tents and bunkers and began to maneuver toward the stricken aircraft.

A second RPG had struck the cockpit causing further shrapnel injuries to the pilots and as the dazed Rangers and aircrew attempted to get to their feet, yet another tore through the Chinook, miraculously not detonating but igniting an oxygen bottle that exploded and set fire to the cabin. AK and PKM fire raked the downed helicopter, punching through the thin sides. An enemy bullet hit and killed door-gunner Sergeant Philip Svitak, tragically hitting him just under his body armor. A second door-gunner, Staff Sergeant Dave Dube, was wounded with a gunshot to his left leg.

Three of the Rangers of Chalk 1 of the Task Force 11 QRF. From the left: Staff Sergeant Ray DePouli, armed with an M4A1 carbine mounting an M68 Aimpoint, Surefire tactical light, and AN/PEQ-2 infrared illuminator; the assistant gunner Private First Class David Gilliam, armed with the M240B general-purpose machine gun; and SAW gunner Specialist Aaron Totten-Lancaster, armed with a collapsible-stock M249 mounting what appears to be an Aimpoint sight, a Surefire light source, and an AN/PEQ-2 illuminator. (US Army)

c.06:10, MARCH 4

RAZOR 01 lands on Takur Ghar; three Rangers are killed

The Chinook pilot, Chief Warrant Officer Greg Calvert, could see three fighters emerge over a large rock some 50m up the slope. He managed to unclip his M4A1 carbine and opened fire on them, driving them back into cover. As he attempted to force open the emergency door, the enemy began firing on him again. As he again tried to grab his M4A1, he realized that an enemy bullet had struck his wrist and virtually severed his hand. Worse still, the round was a tracer and was still impacted in his flesh, burning away.

Three Rangers had made it down the ramp and were firing up the slope, following their training and attempting to suppress the enemy. They quickly killed two nearby fighters – one armed with an RPG-7. Self and Totten-Lancaster (Totten-Lancaster had already suffered fragmentation wounds from an exploding RPG round whilst in the Chinook) made it to the front of the aircraft on the right-hand side and took cover in a slight depression alongside the Chinook's refueling probe. An enemy fighter peered over at them from the rocks directly ahead. Both Americans opened fire, Totten-Lancaster firing short bursts from his SAW and Self firing deliberate aimed shots from his M4A1. The fighter disappeared behind the rock.

Self quickly established that he had lost three of his Rangers in the ambush. Marc Anderson, Brad Crose, and Matt Commons all lay dead. Crose and Commons were both killed as they attempted to race off the ramp as the helicopter landed. Anderson, the team's machine-gunner, had been hit and killed instantly whilst still inside the aircraft. Both of the pilots were wounded multiple times, one of the aircrew was dead, and several others were hurt, including the seriously wounded Dube. The PJs and the 160th SOAR flight medic, Sergeant First Class Cory Lamoreaux, immediately began attempting to stabilize the wounded, despite the bullets punching through the Chinook.

The 160th Air Mission Commander, Chief Warrant Officer Don Tabron, ran down the ramp and joined the Rangers to the side of the Chinook and began firing controlled pairs, conserving his ammunition. On the far side of the aircraft, Chief Warrant Officer Chuck Gant, the co-pilot, had managed despite a ferocious gunshot wound to his left leg to open the emergency door on the left-hand side of the Chinook and roll out into the snow. From there he covered the left side of the helicopter with his M4A1 whilst attempting to get the attention of a medic.

Inside RAZOR 01, Lamoreaux and the PJs continued their work on the wounded. Calvert had been hit by RPG fragments from yet another rocket that had exploded into the helicopter. Despite his wounds, he continued to try and raise communications with the overhead P-3 or F-15Es using his PRC-112 line-of-sight survival radio. The medic and the PJs kept the wounded in the aircraft, hugging the floor as the 2ft-tall ballistic fuel tanks on both sides of the MH-47E provided the best and only protection.

The battle of Takur Ghar

The Rangers began to regroup and Self developed a hasty battle plan. He knew that the helicopter had come down in a slight, horseshoe-shaped depression that saved them from the DShK positioned farther back on

Overleaf
At 06:10, the Chinook known by its callsign of RAZOR 01 landed directly onto the snow-packed peak. As it landed it was engaged in a ferocious volume of gunfire and RPGs from the IMU mujahideen defending the peak. Several mujahideen fighters fired down upon the helicopter from a stone-and-log bunker located at the top of the slope whilst other mujahideen fired from behind the adjacent boulders and attempted to flank the downed helicopter. These mujahideen firing from the bunker were typical of the enemy on Takur Ghar. Most wore the traditional two-piece shalwar kameez with various jackets worn over the top, including commercial cold-weather clothing and US military items (here including a Gore Tex desert-pattern jacket pilfered from the body of Navy SEAL Roberts). The mujahideen were heavily armed with PKM and RPK machine guns, RPG-7s, and various makes of AK assault rifle.

the crest. The enemy was firing down on his men from the higher ground of the peak looking down on the depression and the crashed helicopter. He identified a PKM general-purpose machine gun engaging them from under some trees to his front right, some 60m up the slope. Other mujahideen armed with AKs and RPGs were using the rocks and boulders directly to his front as cover, popping up to fire.

Self decided that the Rangers couldn't risk being pinned down and in his excellent autobiographical account of the battle, *Two Wars*, he mentions recalling his Ranger training at the time – "Return fire and seek cover. Locate the enemy. Suppress the enemy. Attack" (Self 2008: 159). He decided to immediately suppress the enemy firing points and launch a counterattack against the peak. He issued his quick battle orders and all of the Rangers stood up and began firing at both known and suspected enemy positions whilst they bounded forward in subteams – one team firing to suppress whilst the other moved and vice versa.

They made it 15–20m to two small clusters of rocks to the right (southeast) of the downed helicopter until the weight of enemy fire drove them to seek cover. Self's M4A1 malfunctioned and he attempted to clear the stoppage with a cleaning rod that promptly broke. Running back, under fire, to the Chinook's ramp, he managed to grab Crose's M4A1 before dashing back to the marginal safety of the rocks.

At this point in the battle, Totten-Lancaster was in the shallow depression near the aircraft's refueling probe firing his SAW; Self, Walker, and Vance were firing from behind the first pile of rocks; DePouli was firing his carbine from the smaller group of rocks to their right; Gilliam was at the Chinook; and Miceli (minus his SAW, which had been struck by rounds and blown out of his grasp as he exited the Chinook; he was now armed with an M4A1) covered their rear, positioned some 40m behind them on a slight rise.

Totten-Lancaster was ordered to pull back to the rocks so that the Rangers could establish a base of fire with his SAW. As he rolled down the slope towards the rocks, the mujahideen began throwing fragmentation grenades down the slope toward them. Walker responded in kind but could not throw the 50–60m uphill to reach the enemy positions. Another RPG whistled across the ramp of the Chinook. The RPG gunner exposed himself just long enough for DePouli to kill him with several aimed shots.

With the SAW gunner now in position to the left of the larger rocks, DePouli and Self brought Gilliam forward with the M240B, positioning him to the right of DePouli at the smaller group of rocks where the body of a dead mujahideen with an RPG lay. Soon, the M240B was up and firing, suppressing the defenders of the peak. Don Tabron and Sergeant Brian Wilson from the aircrew began ferrying 7.62mm link from the helicopter to Gilliam and as many 5.56mm M4 magazines as they could to pass along to the Rangers.

A blurred image of RAZOR 01 crashlanded on Takur Ghar during the battle. It appears to have been taken from the rocks that Self's Rangers used as cover directly to the right of the helicopter. (US Army)

Becoming frustrated by the grenades being thrown down the slope at them, Walker dashed back to the Chinook and retrieved the one M203 launcher the Rangers had with them – it had been carried by Matt Commons until he had been shot and killed on the ramp. Returning to his position under covering fire from his comrades, Walker began firing 40mm high-explosive grenades up towards the bunker. The first rounds sailed over the peak to explode harmlessly beyond the enemy positions. Walker adjusted his fire and began firing grenades at the boulders, spraying shrapnel over the dug-in defenders.

Self was worried about rear security in case the enemy attempted to flank the static Rangers so he sent Totten-Lancaster's SAW down to Miceli, giving him the firepower to suppress any such attempts. Some 20m behind Self, in a shallow depression in the snow, crouched the Air Force Combat Controller, Sergeant Gabe Brown. Brown had set down his M4A1 and was using his SATCOM radio to attempt to establish communications with any nearby air support, including the pair of F-15Es that were still orbiting overhead.

DePouli and Miceli quickly scouted the right flank to ascertain whether the Rangers could use it as a covered approach to close-assault the peak but found only a sheer drop. Farther down the slope to their rear the pair discovered an enemy position. Both men went in firing but the position was at that time unoccupied. They found an old SPG-9 recoilless rifle (without any ammunition), a covered sleeping position, and a specially constructed prayer space for mujahideen fighters. They also recovered an American rucksack and an MBITR. The handheld radio was marked with the callsign of its owner – "RED 1S." Self knew it was a SEAL callsign. They had found the first evidence of the missing man, Roberts.

At 07:18, Brown had the first close air support (CAS) on-station, the pair of orbiting F-15E Strike Eagles. Self, Brown, and Vance decided against using bombs at this stage fearing the "danger close" range and instead Brown instructed the Twister callsigns to use their 20mm cannon on strafing

07:18, MARCH 4

First close air support arrives

Ranger Specialist Anthony Miceli manning the eastern security position during the battle. He carries Totten-Lancaster's SAW as his own had been struck by enemy fire as he exited the Chinook. (US Army)

runs. The Strike Eagles flew in over the peak, launching flares against any potential SAM threat, and spotted the helicopter. Vance didn't like their initial angle of attack so the attack heading was adjusted as Brown spoke directly to the pilots. This would be the first time in combat history that F-15Es would conduct gun runs in support of troops in contact. The pair of F-15Es flew in again on the new heading to ensure the G-FACs (Ground Forward Air Controllers) – Brown and Vance – were happy with their direction of attack before swinging around for their actual attack run.

At 07:20, the lead F-15E swept in, its 20mm cannon blazing. The rounds landed short by some 20m. Brown corrected and the F-15E swung in again. At 07:21, with the aim corrected, the 20mm rounds smashed into the enemy bunker and treeline. With good effects on target, the F-15Es banked around again and conducted a third gun run at 07:23. Each gun run had expended anywhere between 80 and 180 rounds of 20mm cannon ammunition.

The enemy on the peak were momentarily dazed and suppressed and the CAS proved a vital morale boost for the embattled Rangers. The F-15Es went off-station to refuel whilst Brown lined up further air support in the form of a pair of F-16CG Fighting Falcons that had just come on-station. He was also contacted by JULIET, the Delta AFO team, which had good views of Takur Ghar and told him about several enemy fighters hunkered down behind the first bunker. Self ordered him to call in the F-16CGs. His plan was for the Falcons to suppress the enemy again with cannon fire before he launched a ground assault with his Rangers.

At approximately 08:01, the first F-16CG Clash callsign rolled into the attack heading, firing its 20mm cannon. As the F-16CG pilots were not yet conditioned to the terrain, and doubtless fearful of friendly fire, the 20mm rounds missed. The pilots came around on another pass and this time the rounds were closer to the target. By the third pass, the big cannon shells were finally hitting the treeline and boulders.

The pair of F-16CGs conducted four gun runs in total before they declared "Winchester" on their ammunition states ("Winchester" is a USAF

The peak of Takur Ghar with the downed MH-47E, RAZOR 01, visible on the slope. The bunker complex and treeline are directly ahead and to the right of the Chinook. (DOD)

brevity code indicating running out of ammunition or ordnance much as the brevity code "Bingo" indicates a low fuel state). It was enough for Self and judging the enemy suppressed, he ordered the ground assault.

At about 08:07 Gilliam, with Wilson now acting as his assistant gunner, opened fire with the M240B providing covering fire as Self, Walker, Vance, and DePouli stood up and began firing, walking up the slope in the knee-deep snow. The enemy were evidently keeping their heads down and no fire was returned as the Rangers moved as quickly as they could toward the peak. They had covered about half the 55m distance when a mujahideen under the trees fired two quick bursts at them from a PKM emplaced there, before disappearing into a fighting position behind the tree. Self then realized that what they had all assumed was simply fallen logs and foliage that the enemy were using for cover was, in fact, a fortified bunker.

Self ordered the Rangers to withdraw in bounds, firing to suppress as they moved. They didn't have enough men to start clearing bunkers and other prepared positions. Nor did they have the right sort of weaponry; they carried no M72 LAWs or AT-4s – handheld rockets that excelled at "bunker busting." As Self commented: "If the enemy bunker was built as well as it looked, then our 7.62mm machine-gun rounds would have little effect on it. And even after the jets' gun runs, it appeared that some of the enemy fighters had survived. I needed heavier weapons. We had failed to bring our anti-tank missiles along with us – a costly oversight" (Self 2008: 183).

Chalk 2

After RAZOR 01 was shot down on the peak, RAZOR 02 with Canon's team was ordered to return to Gardez until the situation on the mountain became clearer. Canon and his Rangers were understandably frustrated. At Gardez, they were met on the strip by the SEAL commander, Hyder, who joined them in the Chinook, to await the order to return to the trapped Rangers. The pilots were finally supplied with the coordinates of an offset HLZ and at 07:00, they lifted off.

Halfway to the HLZ, they were instructed to go into a holding pattern whilst the first F-15E gun runs on the peak were completed. Soon after, they were cleared to land. MAKO 30 was now in contact with RAZOR 02 and gave the helicopter the coordinates of an offset HLZ closer to the SEALs. Chalk 2 landed at approximately 08:32.

Canon immediately contacted Self and informed him they were on the ground and would be moving to link up with Chalk 1. The only difficulty was that the location of the HLZ meant Canon and his men would need to climb up almost 3,000ft at a seventy-degree incline with their heavy body armor, ammunition, and weapons, including the 12.5kg M240B. Hyder had other ideas. He asked the Rangers to accompany him to link up with the SEALs of MAKO 30 first before attempting to scale the mountain.

Canon contacted Self, who was incredulous – he and his team were in contact with the enemy and needed reinforcements to storm the bunkers. "He can go to his guys. They're fine. We're still getting shot at up here. Tell him I need you here" Self told Canon (Self 2008: 186). Hyder set off by

Overleaf

Captain Nate Self soon organized his surviving Rangers to attempt to suppress the enemy defenders. Only once this was done could they attempt to assault the bunker complex on the peak. Self had his Rangers split into two teams – himself, Vance, Totten-Lancaster, and Walker taking cover behind a cluster of rocks some 15m from the crashed Chinook, and DePouli and Gilliam manning the sole M240B general-purpose machine gun on their right flank behind a second, smaller cluster of rocks. Miceli, unseen in this illustration, was at this point protecting the eastern flank behind the Rangers to guard against an enemy attack from that direction.

himself to link up with his SEALs leaving the Rangers of Chalk 2 to begin the climb. Self was quoted by author Sean Naylor: "I didn't want him to come up. They're Navy. They do things differently. We knew that from working with them previously" (quoted in Naylor 2005: 353).

Self had an M203 flare round fired so that Canon could spot their direction. Canon and Chalk 2 couldn't see it. Passing their grid reference to Self, Canon realized that Chalk 2 were climbing in from behind Chalk 1's positions rather than from the western flank as Canon had assumed. Self provided Canon with further directions and Chalk 2 set out. They estimated the climb would take them 45 minutes. Chalk 2 should arrive directly to the east of Chalk 1 and the downed helicopter.

Hyder met up with the SEALs, realizing now how badly wounded two of them were. He developed a plan that would see MAKO 30 walk down the mountain to another HLZ where they would await extraction. Along the way, they saw an apparently unarmed Afghan running down the mountain whom Hyder shot and killed, suspecting the man was an enemy mortar spotter. With the seriously wounded SEALs rapidly deteriorating in the cold, Hyder was forced to find shelter in a tree-lined draw some 1,500m farther down the slope and attempted to treat his wounded men.

The final battle

Back up on the top of the mountain, a mujahideen mortar crew had begun to bracket the peak with 82mm rounds. With Canon's team still some time away, Self needed to do something before the mortars found their range. He decided to call in a bomb run on the bunker. Brown made contact with a pair of circling F-15Es that were carrying GBU-12 Paveway II 500lb bombs. As Brown lined up the CAS, Miceli shouted that he could see three enemy walking in the valley to the east. Fearing they may have been controlling the mortar fire, Miceli opened fire with his SAW but the 5.56mm rounds simply didn't have the power to hit targets beyond their effective range.

Moments later, at 08:45, the lead F-15E, Twister Five Two, came in on its attack run. The bomb landed on the far side of the peak with a deep rumble. Brown and Vance brought in the next aircraft, an F-16CG, which placed its bomb closer to the peak. The two air controllers brought the bombs ever closer on each run. The final GBU-12 impacted the closest, landing just shy of the peak and sending shrapnel into the bunker and trees. With the potential for fratricide, Self wasn't prepared to call in the bombs any closer to his position.

Brown and Vance were constantly supported by an Australian SASR patrol from Task Force 64 manning

08:32, MARCH 4

RAZOR 02/Chalk 2 lands on Takur Ghar

Ranger Specialist Randy J. Pazder mans his M240B whilst maintaining security to the east. This photo appears to have been taken just after the counterattack by mujahideen elements from the ridge visible in the middle ground of the image. (US Army)

an OP on a mountain peak some 4km to the southwest. The SASR patrol, with an embedded US Air Force Combat Controller, had excellent "eyes on" Takur Ghar and continually fed updates on mujahideen movements to the trapped Rangers. Brigadier Duncan Lewis, the former commander of Australia's Special Operations Command, stated in a press conference in March 2002:

> A group of Australians located in an observation post overlooking the site of the downed aircraft and the stranded US soldiers was the only friendly force in the area – members of this patrol were able to view al Qaeda fighters massing for an assault on the downed US helicopter. The Australian patrol accurately coordinated multiple air strikes to prevent the al Qaeda forces overrunning the survivors. (ADF SOCOMD 2002)

The Rangers and aircrew identified another possible HLZ, a small ledge protected by a steep ridge that would provide cover from the mortars, some 150m to the east. Once they moved the wounded to the shelf, Self hoped an extraction helicopter could be brought in. Brown was in contact with the operator of an orbiting CIA RQ-1 Predator UAV that gave Self an idea. Some of the Predators had been recently armed with a pair of AGM-114 Hellfire II antitank missiles. Brown confirmed that this particular Predator was indeed armed and Self ordered a strike on the bunker – the first recorded use of the Predator as close air support.

At about 09:44, the first Hellfire missed, striking somewhere to their north. The controller lined up another shot and launched its second Hellfire into the trees and hit the bunker dead on. Self considered another assault with his small team but dismissed the idea and decided to await the arrival of Canon's Chalk 2. Canon reported that they were now taking ineffective mortar fire, apparently from the same mortar team that had been firing on the peak. Canon's Rangers ditched as much non-essential gear as they could to lighten their load and speed up the climb, including the ceramic back plates from their RBA (Ranger Body Armor).

At approximately 10:20, after a physically and mentally draining climb, the Rangers of Chalk 2 arrived on the top of the mountain and linked up with Chalk 1. They also made a disturbing discovery as they arrived – a discarded American Pro-Tec helmet with a single bullet hole and blood inside it. They also found a Nalgene water bottle with "Fifi," Roberts' nickname, written on it. Now that the two Ranger elements had linked up, Self wasted no time in planning another assault on the peak. He quickly issued his orders.

The second machine-gun team – Specialists Randy Pazder and Omar Vela – was placed next to Gilliam and Wilson as they had the best arcs to cover the advance. The plan was straightforward – whilst the two M240Bs commanded by Canon fired suppressive fires on the peak, Staff Sergeant Harper Wilmoth and a fire team from Chalk 2 would advance in bounds with Walker leading a second fire team. DePouli, Miceli, and Totten-Lancaster would provide flank security.

Some of the Rangers of Chalk 2. From left to right: Staff Sergeant Harper Wilmoth; Specialist Oscar Escano; Specialist Randy Pazder; Specialist Jonas Polson; Sergeant Patrick George; Specialist Omar Vela; Specialist Chris Cunningham. (US Army)

Upon Self's order, at 11:02 the machine-gunners opened fire and the Rangers charged up the slope as quickly as the snow would allow. The fire teams reached the first bunker – its occupants having been killed by the Predator – and killed an enemy fighter hiding behind it. Discovering the second bunker and the roughly hewn trench lines on the far side of the peak, the Rangers went into clearance mode, posting fragmentation grenades and spraying the trenches with automatic fire. Canon, who had now joined the assault elements, posted a grenade into the second bunker that set off a number of RPG rounds stored there, destroying the bunker and knocking Canon off his feet.

Canon also located the missing man, whose fall from the Chinook some eight hours earlier had triggered the Rangers' mission. Neil Roberts' body was discovered near the boulders and under the tree the Rangers had nicknamed the "Bonsai." He had a fatal head wound. Initially the Rangers were concerned they had killed the American with the air strikes or their small-arms fire although this was later proven to not have been the case. The body of Air Force Combat Controller John Chapman was also found in the first bunker, puzzling the Rangers as they were unaware MAKO 30 had lost a second man.

Wilmoth's fire team continued around past the enemy positions and cleared up towards the southern edge of the peak where they discovered another enemy fighter hiding near the far end of the boulders. He was rapidly engaged and killed. The DShK position encountered by MAKO 30 earlier had been abandoned. At 11:14, Staff Sergeant Wilmoth declared the objective secure – the Rangers had finally cleared the peak.

The fate of Chapman

Exactly what happened to Technical Sergeant John A. "Chappy" Chapman remains open to considerable conjecture. What appears to have occurred was that at 05:52, some 30 minutes after the SEALs of MAKO 30 had broken contact and withdrawn from the peak, an RQ-1 Predator UAV spotted an unusual and disturbing series of events on the mountain.

The Predator's camera picked up an unknown individual, presumably a mujahideen fighter, emerge from cover and cross in front of the first bunker whose initial three occupants had been killed by Chapman earlier that morning. This individual appeared to be trying to flank whoever was now occupying that bunker.

Another enemy fighter emerged from the east of the bunker and fired an RPG rocket at the bunker. The first individual, still attempting to flank the bunker, was then killed by small-arms fire from within the bunker itself. The fighter carrying the RPG then ended the short firefight by assaulting the bunker and presumably killing whoever was inside.

Chapman's body was recovered not outside the first bunker where he had first fallen but inside the bunker, lending weight to the theory that perhaps Chapman was not actually dead when the SEALs withdrew. Perhaps only unconscious and weakened from blood loss (later coronial evidence declared that his gunshot wound would have likely been immediately fatal), Chapman may have made it into the bunker to await rescue until spotted by the enemy fighters and after a valiant defense, he was finally shot and killed.

Other possible explanations include the hypothesis that somehow Roberts was not killed when initially thought but that he fought on. The location of his body, however, tallied with where he fell after he was brutally executed. Chapman's body could have been dragged into the bunker by an enemy fighter or blown into the bunker by the repeated air strikes conducted in support of the Ranger QRF.

The puzzling incident could also be explained by a friendly-fire clash between mujahideen fighters, caused by the chaos and confusion of the battle on the mountain. Weighing the probabilities, this is perhaps the most likely explanation. Whoever the mysterious shooter in the bunker was, he was finally killed less than a minute before RAZOR 01 arrived on the peak at 06:07.

11:14, MARCH 4

Takur Ghar secured

Getting off the mountain

Now that the mountaintop had been cleared of all enemy forces and secured, Self's efforts focused on the most pressing matter at hand – evacuating the seriously wounded before their deteriorating state and the cold weather could claim more victims. Vance established communications with the Task Force 11 headquarters element at Masirah whilst the Rangers and aircrew used Skedco litters, carried by the Air Force PJs for exactly this contingency, to drag the seriously wounded up the slope toward the peak where Ranger medic, Sergeant Matt LaFrenz, had established his casualty collection point (CCP).

At 11:31, as Vance relayed that the HLZ was "ice," sudden small-arms fire rang out from the south-southeast behind the downed Chinook. Self and his men quickly identified that the fire, likely from a PKM, was originating from a narrow shelf several hundred meters behind them, apparently using a cave complex to attempt to flank the Rangers. Both M240B gunners began returning fire whilst Brown called for immediate CAS. Self established his Rangers in two defensive positions – the first was around the bunker complex on the peak and the second around the rear of the Chinook to protect the casualties whilst they were being moved to the CCP. An RPG landed near the large rocks the Rangers had earlier used for cover and exploded up the slope.

Brown and Jaguar One Two, the Air Force Combat Controller embedded with an Australian SASR patrol some 4km to the southwest, now coordinated a B-52 bomber strike on the ledge but the bombs missed. Brown then brought in a pair of US Navy F/A-18 Hornets that dropped a 500lb GBU-12 with astounding accuracy, silencing the enemy fire at 12:06.

The enemy fire had caused two more friendly casualties. One of the PJs, Jason Cunningham, had been hit along with the 160th SOAR flight medic, Cory Lamoreaux. Both had been seriously wounded. The Rangers and aircrew again began moving the casualties up toward the CCP – they now had five seriously wounded requiring litters (stretchers) and six bodies to move to the safety of the peak. The only positive news at this point was that a French Mirage had managed to destroy the 82mm mortar team whose fire had plagued the Rangers all day.

A Marine AH-1W Cobra takes off from USS *Bonhomme Richard* in support of Operation *Anaconda* on March 4. At times the number of CAS assets over Takur Ghar created severe command-and-control difficulties. (US Marine Corps)

Brown again requested clarification on when the wounded could be extracted and was told that a Task Force 11 extraction package including SEAL and Ranger reinforcements and Apache gunship cover would soon be launching from Gardez. Self didn't need the reinforcements – he needed the urgent casualties to be evacuated and was content to wait until night fell to finally extract the lightly wounded and able-bodied.

At around 15:30, another group of enemy appeared on the same ridge to their south-southeast – again both M240B gunners suppressed them whilst Brown vectored in a pair of Navy F-14 Tomcats. One 500lb bomb went "dumb" (a term for when a smart guided bomb such as a Paveway or JDAM loses its targeting guidance) and landed just 30m down the slope from the Chinook, narrowly avoiding causing further injuries. The next bombs luckily landed on target.

With no concrete timing for an extraction of the wounded, Self and his men were becoming increasingly frustrated. LaFrenz was adamant on his casualty status – they would have two further KIA (Killed in Action) unless a helicopter soon arrived. Self reiterated the casualty status to the TOC at Masirah and was met with empty reassurances until eventually Trebon came onto the radio and informed him that no medical extraction would now be conducted until nightfall.

Cunningham, shot in the abdomen, rapidly deteriorated until finally at 18:08, he died. LaFrenz attempted to resuscitate him to no avail. Self reported to the TOC that his casualty count was now seven KIA. Finally at 20:00, two AC-130s came on-station to cover the extraction. Fifteen minutes later, the extraction force reported that they could see the Rangers' infrared strobe marking the HLZ. With Apache, Predator, and A-10 cover, and with the AC-130s scanning the surrounding peaks and ridges for threats, the first MH-47E of the extraction package set down on Takur Ghar.

As a final hurdle, the lead MH-47E, tasked with extracting the casualties, landed in the wrong direction – with its tail, and ramp, facing down the hill, rather than toward the casualties at the peak – and the SEAL security element that arrived upon it did nothing to assist the exhausted Rangers, Special Tactics, and Nightstalker survivors with loading their wounded. Most of the remaining Rangers of Chalk 1 also loaded onto the first Chinook with their wounded. Finally the first extraction Chinook lifted off, heading to Bagram.

The second MH-47E touched down and the dead were loaded on board. Canon's Chalk 2 members walked up the ramp and collapsed inside. Last aboard were Vance and Self. A third Chinook managed to precariously land one rear wheel on the narrow ridge MAKO 30 were sheltering upon and the SEALs carried their wounded up the ramp. At about 20:20, the last US servicemen on Takur Ghar were finally extracted.

The battle of Takur Ghar had lasted approximately 17 hours. Seven men died on the mountain – one SEAL, one Combat Controller, three Rangers, one Nightstalker, and one Pararescue Jumper. The majority of the survivors suffered wounds, some light and some life threatening. Cory Lamoreaux, the 160th flight medic, recovered from his wounds and returned to the

20:00, MARCH 4

AC-130s arrive to cover the extraction

20:20, MARCH 4

Extraction complete

Nightstalkers. "Brett," the MAKO 30 SEAL, also recovered fully. Another SEAL, "Turbo," lost his leg below the knee. RAZOR 01's pilot, Greg Calvert, had his severed hand reattached, and eventually returned to the Nightstalkers to again fly Chinooks.

ANACONDA ORDER OF BATTLE, MARCH 2002

Task Force Dagger

Commander: Colonel John Mulholland, 5th Special Forces Group (Airborne)

5th Special Forces Group (Airborne)

B Company, 2nd Battalion, 160th Special Operations Aviation Regiment (Airborne)

Special Tactics Squadron elements, USAF Special Operations

Afghan Military Forces:

Commander Zia Lodin (Task Force Hammer)

Commander Kamel Khan (Task Force Anvil)

Commander Zakim Khan (Task Force Anvil)

Task Force Rakkasan

Commander: Colonel Frank Wiercinski, 3rd Brigade, 101st Airborne Division (Air Assault)

1st Battalion, 187th Infantry, 101st Airborne Division (Air Assault)

2nd Battalion, 187th Infantry, 101st Airborne Division (Air Assault)

1st Battalion, 87th Infantry, 10th Mountain Division

Task Force Commando

Commander: Colonel Kevin Wilkerson, 2nd Brigade, 10th Mountain Division

4th Battalion, 31st Infantry, 10th Mountain Division

3rd Battalion, Princess Patricia's Canadian Light Infantry

Task Force 64

Commander: Lieutenant Colonel Rowan Tink, Special Air Service Regiment

Task Force K-Bar

Commander: Captain Robert Harward, US Navy SEALs

Task Force Bowie

Commander: Brigadier General Gary Harrell, US Army Special Operations Command

Task Force 11 Advanced Force Operations

Commander: Lieutenant Colonel Pete Blaber, US Army 1st Special Forces Operational Detachment – Delta

MAKO 30 – personnel and armament

"Slab" (team leader): SR-25 plus stand-alone grenade launcher, probably cut-down M79

"Brett": Mk 43 Mod 0

"Fifi" (Petty Officer First Class Neil Roberts): Minimi SPW or Mk 46 Mod 0

"Kyle": SR-25 plus stand-alone grenade launcher, probably cut-down M79

"Randy": SR-25 plus stand-alone grenade launcher, probably cut-down M79

"Thor" (Grey Fox SIGINT operator): probably M4A1 ("Thor" was offloaded at Gardez after 04:34 and did not return to Takur Ghar)

"Turbo": M4A1, possibly with M203

Technical Sergeant John A. Chapman USAF (combat controller): M4A1

The end of *Anaconda*

Only one of the original three AFO teams now remained in the valley – the Army Delta JULIET team. INDIA and MAKO 31 had been eventually withdrawn as their supplies dwindled. INDIA had been replaced by a new

Chalk 1 – personnel and armament

Captain Nate Self (platoon leader): M4A1

Staff Sergeant Ray DePouli (1st Squad leader): M4A1

Sergeant Joshua Walker (1st Squad Alpha Fire Team leader): M4A1

Sergeant Bradley Crose (1st Squad Bravo Fire Team leader): M4A1

Specialist Anthony Miceli (Alpha SAW gunner): M249

Specialist Aaron Totten-Lancaster (Bravo SAW gunner): M249

Private First Class Matthew Commons (Alpha grenadier) M4A1/M203

Specialist Marc Anderson (machine-gunner attached from Weapons Squad): M240B

Private First Class David Gilliam (assistant M240B gunner from Weapons Squad): M4A1

Staff Sergeant Kevin Vance USAF (attached ETAC): M4A1

Attached US Air Force Special Tactics Squadrons operators:

Staff Sergeant Gabe Brown USAF (combat controller): M4A1

Senior Airman Jason Cunningham USAF (Pararescue Jumper): M4A1

Technical Sergeant Keary Miller USAF (Pararescue Jumper): M4A1

Chalk 2 – personnel and armament

Staff Sergeant Arin Canon (Weapons Squad leader): M4A1

Staff Sergeant Harper Wilmoth (2nd Squad leader): M4A1

Sergeant Eric Stebner (2nd Squad Alpha Fire Team leader): M4A1

Sergeant Patrick George (2nd Squad Bravo Fire Team leader): M4A1, probably with M203

Specialist Jonas Polson (Alpha SAW gunner): M249

Specialist Chris Cunningham (Bravo SAW Gunner): M249

Specialist Oscar Escano (Alpha grenadier): M4A1/M203

Specialist Randy Pazder (machine-gunner attached from Weapons Squad): M240B

Specialist Omar Vela (assistant M240B gunner from Weapons Squad): M4A1

Sergeant Matt LaFrenz (platoon medic): M4A1

RAZOR 01 air crew

Chief Warrant Officer Class 5 Don Tabron (air mission commander)

Chief Warrant Officer Class 4 Chuck Gant (pilot)

Chief Warrant Officer Class 3 Greg Calvert (co-pilot)

Sergeant Philip Svitak (engineer/door-gunner)

Staff Sergeant David Dube (flight engineer/door-gunner)

Sergeant Sean Ludwig (crew chief/ramp-gunner)

Sergeant Brian "Jed" Wilson (crew chief/ramp-gunner)

Sergeant First Class Cory Lamoreaux (flight medic)

element, MAKO 22, whilst another new SEAL element, MAKO 21, established a position some 2km east of JULIET. JULIET was eventually withdrawn on March 5 and the team left their hide site the same way they had come in – on their Polaris ATVs.

As the Rakkasans fought through the valley, they conducted over 129 cave clearances and 40 building clearances, and eliminated 22 mujahideen fortifications. By March 4, the enemy appeared largely beaten. For political reasons, Afghan forces were to be introduced into the valley as a belated attempt to "put an Afghan face" on the operation. This inevitably stalled as tribal issues between AMF commanders flared up.

Whilst the "Afghan solution" was being worked out, the 4-31st from the 10th Mountain and the 3rd Battalion of the Princess Patricia's Canadian Light Infantry were inserted into the Shahikot to reinforce the Rakkasans. Eventually the AMF settled their differences and with SF and AFO support, they advanced into the Shahikot with T-55 tanks in support on March 12, signaling the end of major operations in the valley. Four days later, CENTCOM announced Operation *Anaconda* over.

The mujahideen had been driven from the Shahikot Valley or they were killed where they stood. Estimates of enemy dead range from source to source with little agreement although a total of anywhere between 200 and 500 dead seems most likely. Coalition forces lost eight men killed in action – seven on Takur Ghar. They also suffered some 80 wounded, many amongst the men of Task Force Rakkasan.

A postscript – Operation *Wolverine*

On March 17, 2002, Task Force 11 received time-sensitive intelligence that a possible HVT was travelling within a convoy of al-Qaeda fighters who

A member of the 1st Battalion, 187th Infantry mans a tripod-mounted .50-caliber M2 heavy machine gun overlooking the Shahikot Valley on March 4. An airstrike has just been conducted on the village of Babukhel. (US Army)

were attempting to escape by vehicle from the Shahikot and into neighboring Pakistan. An RQ-1 Predator UAV had the convoy under surveillance and reported back to Bagram that the convoy consisted of three Sports Utility Vehicles (SUVs) of the type al-Qaeda HVTs preferred – a white Toyota 4Runner, a second 4Runner painted red, and a Toyota Hilux pickup truck carrying a large security element of hooded gunmen.

The Task Force 11 force element assigned the mission included SEAL operators from DEVGRU, commanded by Slab, to conduct the actual vehicle stop, with a mixed force of Rangers from both the 1st and 3rd Battalions to act as the QRF in case a security cordon needed to be established. The DEVGRU operators and an assigned Combat Search And Rescue (CSAR) team from Air Force Special Tactics boarded three MH-47Es whilst the Rangers climbed aboard a pair of MH-60G Pave Hawks. The five helicopters launched from Bagram in the early morning, flying low and fast toward the target area.

The combined flight arrived over the location and spotted the convoy driving at speed up a narrow wadi (dry stream-bed). The helicopters approached the convoy from behind before the lead MH-47E overtook the vehicles and performed a fast turn and flared to land in their path. The SUVs abruptly stopped and the gunmen raced from their vehicles to find cover.

With the first sign of hostile intent as the vehicles' occupants shouldered their AKs, the left-side door-gunner of the landed Chinook opened fire with his M134 minigun. The second MH-47E flew along above the stalled convoy and added to the fire, raking the vehicles with both minigun and M60D fire. The DEVGRU operators also opened fire from the helicopter, having earlier received permission to jettison the Plexiglass side windows in the helicopter.

As the second Chinook peeled away, the third flew over the convoy, its door-gunner opening fire with his minigun until it abruptly suffered a stoppage. A Nightstalker flight medic and former Ranger quickly grabbed his M4A1 and managed to engage and kill the driver of the third SUV as he attempted to reverse out of the kill zone. This third helicopter then swung around and landed behind the crest of a small hill overlooking the wadi, its cargo of operators racing down the ramp and taking up firing positions above the enemy fighters.

The second Chinook turned and flew farther back up the wadi as a fourth vehicle had been spotted, trailing the convoy. Uncertain of hostile intent but unable to land the big helicopter, the Chinook hovered 20ft above the SUV, its left-side minigun trained on the vehicle. A female emerged into the rotorwash with a child in her arms whilst the others exited the vehicle and sat by the side of the road, apparently unarmed. The Chinook dropped off its team of operators who conducted an extensive search of the people and their vehicle. With nothing incriminating found they were held until the main operation was complete and then released to go on their way.

Back at the ambush site, both teams of DEVGRU operators were now firing down on the enemy fighters in a vicious crossfire. As fighters attempted to move to cover or return fire, they were engaged and killed. In minutes the contact was over and the operators moved down into the wadi to secure the dead and wounded. Of the 18 enemy fighters in the three vehicles, 16 had been killed outright and two seriously wounded and captured. The fighters appeared to be a mix of IMU Uzbeks and Chechens and "Afghan Arabs," and were well equipped and supplied. One wore a makeshift suicide vest of fragmentation grenades concealed in a harness under his arms whilst another, a potential HVT, had disguised himself within a female burkha.

The operators recovered a US-made sound suppressor, a number of US-manufactured fragmentation grenades of a lot issued to Task Force 11, and a Garmin handheld GPS inscribed with the name Gordon. This briefly made news as suggestions were made that this was a device once owned by Master Sergeant Gary Gordon, a Delta sniper killed in Mogadishu, Somalia, in 1993. The GPS was later traced to one of the crew of RAZOR 01.

ANALYSIS AND CONCLUSIONS

The battle of Takur Ghar, and Operation *Anaconda* itself, proved to be salutary lessons for the US military. Many of the lessons learnt from March 2002 have contributed to the successful outcome of similar operations in both Afghanistan and Iraq over the past ten years. They range from technological issues to command and control, and touch on the military's need, at least in 2002, to relearn many of the successes and failings of the last great unconventional war, Vietnam.

One of the key operational successes was obviously the introduction of covert observation posts around the valley to identify and target enemy forces. SOF from both the AFO and Task Force K-Bar were able to infiltrate through extremely difficult terrain, at night, and in blizzard conditions, to establish OPs undetected in the enemy heartland. Apart from the MAKO 30 infiltration, these teams remained hidden in the most trying of environments and passed vital intelligence and targeting information back to their headquarters.

Once *Anaconda* was launched, these SOF transitioned to guiding in close air support that undoubtedly saved many lives amongst the men of Task Force Rakkasan. They also hindered the enemy's ability to withdraw or reinforce their forces in the valley. The wildly successful SOF mission was a testament to the impressive skills, training and combat experience of these world-class units. Little can be said to detract from their success.

Technology

Technology was both a tremendous advantage and, when overly relied upon, a terrible hindrance. Communications systems, in particular the SATCOM radios equipping both the Nightstalker MH-47Es and the Spectre gunships, suffered multiple failures when they were needed most. Confusion around communication protocols, for instance with the BOSSMAN AWACS, led to a lack of situational awareness for aircrew, ground troops, and their commanders.

The SEALs' reliance on using their attached USAF Combat Controller to handle radio duties meant that when Chapman was taken out of the fight they were forced to use their line-of-sight MBITRs. Hampered by both range and power, the MBITRs only allowed the SEALs to impart important messages via relays. In the confusion of the initial stages of the battle on the peak, reliable long-range radio systems in tandem with common radio protocols could have had a major effect on the battle.

Firepower was also impacted when key weapons systems became unavailable. Chief amongst these were the door-gun-mounted M134 miniguns, which experienced multiple stoppages before finally failing due to a lack of AC electrical power. Had the miniguns on RAZOR 04 still been operable after the crash landing, they may have been able to provide suppressive fires as the Ranger QRF debussed. Nightstalker airframes now feature battery backup power for their miniguns.

The lack of light antiarmor or bunker-busting munitions carried by the Rangers meant that they became entirely reliant upon close air support to destroy enemy strongpoints on the peak. However, no combat leader goes into action with all the equipment he desires and the QRF was necessarily structured more around fast insertion and extraction missions than prolonged gunfights.

The light 5.56mm caliber of the majority of the Ranger's small arms may have also had an effect on both the terminal ballistics against enemy fighters wearing heavy cold-weather clothing, and their penetrative power against fighters in the bunkers and treeline. The short barrels of the M4A1 carbines also meant that the 5.56mm cartridges rapidly lost velocity; their M240B general-purpose machine guns had no such handicap, firing the heavier 7.62mm bullet, and were decisive in both holding back the enemy and suppressing their positions for the final assault.

Battlefield sensor technology, as used by the Spectre crews, was sometimes problematic. The fact that sophisticated infrared cameras could be defeated by a combination of cold temperatures and blankets used to cover enemy fighters, is particularly worrisome; likewise, the reported failures to identify Roberts with his IR beacon before he was captured and killed.

Several authoritative accounts, including a JSOC investigation, pointed to an over-reliance by the ground forces on these sensor systems. Technological advances over the following decade thankfully addressed many of the issues with such equipment, and the AC-130 aircrews continued to provide lifesaving fire support to Coalition ground forces in Afghanistan.

The advent of unmanned aerial vehicles, or drones, has been a revolution in ISTAR (Intelligence, Surveillance, Target Acquisition and Reconnaissance), allowing commanders to understand the battlespace in real time. With all of its advantages, UAV technology can give the force commander almost too much awareness, or at least perceived awareness. As evidenced by the attempted rescue of Roberts, leadership in remote locations, far from

The remains of RAZOR 01, the MH-47E which transported Chalk 1 of the Ranger QRF to the summit of Takur Ghar. The stranded helicopter had been "denied from the air" by an airstrike after all Ranger and SEAL personnel had been safely extracted. Note the lack of snow on the mountain – this photo was taken over a month after the battle, on April 17, 2002, after the winter snow had melted away. Note that the MH-47E's refuelling probe is still largely intact. (Getty Images)

the physical battlefield can be tempted to overrule the troops on the ground and micro-manage the fight. The innovation of arming UAV platforms, though, has added a welcome capability to their use. Self's Rangers were perhaps the first US ground forces to experience this advantage when CIA Hellfires were fired from an orbiting Predator platform.

Command and control

The combat effectiveness of both the SEALs and the Rangers on Takur Ghar was constrained by conflicting command and control and micro-management. From the initial pressure to insert MAKO 30 against basic tactical common sense, to the tragic delays in allowing helicopter evacuation of the wounded, second-guessing and overruling the soldiers on the ground plagued the entire operation. Trebon, although highly experienced in special-operations aviation, had little operational understanding when dealing with land-based special operations. Nor did he have any experience in classic infantry war-fighting, which the situation on Takur Ghar soon became.

The appointment of Trebon to command Task Force 11 proved to be a challenge for all elements involved in the fight. A far more logical choice would have been the vastly experienced Brigadier General Gary Harrell, who was already in theater leading Task Force Bowie, or either the commander of Delta or DEVGRU. The personal animosity between Trebon and the Army AFO commander, Blaber, negatively impacted upon the management of the AFO effort in the valley. If the AFO commander's advice had been followed, the battle of Takur Ghar, and the deaths of seven special operators, may have been avoided.

Interservice politics between Navy and Army SOF also played their part, highlighted by Task Force Blue forcing the AFO out of their communications loop. By establishing this back channel, the Navy SOF effectively cut themselves off from valuable advice from Army SF, CIA, and AFO who knew the terrain and enemy displacements intimately. The driving reason for the hasty inclusion of the Task Force Blue teams, and Trebon's insistence that command of AFO be handed over to a Navy commander, appears to have been based more on a perceived need to "blood" the SEALs operationally than in any valid tactical reason.

The existing AFO teams in the valley were conducting their mission flawlessly and could have maintained their positions for several further days. Despite being low on some supplies, the teams felt that they could "stay in the fight." Covert resupply was another option – AFO understood the terrain and could have conducted such a resupply as needed.

There is little criticism that can be leveled at the individual Navy SEAL operators who performed bravely in exceedingly difficult circumstances. Many commentators have, however, made reference to the institutional attitude of Navy SOF with its insistence on encroaching into land-based, traditionally Army activities such as the SOF support of *Anaconda* which has long caused additional friction between the services.

Whilst Army Special Forces have generally begun their careers as infantrymen, often later volunteering for the Airborne before joining the Ranger Regiment, then ultimately passing the Special Forces "Q" Course, operators from Delta have the additional step of the Operator's Course that most attempt from the ranks of the Rangers or Special Forces. Critics argue that the SEALs do not have this same background in core infantry skills and thus when a direct-action mission goes wrong, the SEALs do not have those core skills to fall back upon, whereas a Delta or Special Forces operator can immediately transition back to being an infantryman and fight a conventional infantry fight.

Task Force 11's insistence on using black SOF assets may have led to the command ignoring a pair of Air Force HH-60G Pave Hawk rescue helicopters which were less than 15 minutes' flying time away and could have conducted a specialist recovery mission to extract the seriously wounded. Captain Self repeatedly advised that the landing zone was safe and other SOF OPs were negating the enemy's ability to reinforce the peak.

Anaconda

The overall operation, *Anaconda*, faced a number of similar issues but obviously on a far larger scale. Principal among these was the oft-reported poor communication between the Air Force and the Army with regard to the pre–H-Hour bombardment and preparatory fires. Much of the blame falls on the different planning processes used by the two services – the Army has a more streamlined approach whilst Air Force policies at the time of *Anaconda* forced a more rigorous and lengthy approach.

Elements of the plan were also developed in isolation of any Air Force input, which later led to the difficulties experienced. Air Force General T. Michael Moseley, in command of the air component, was only briefed on February 25. He commented in an internal USAF report into *Anaconda*: "Had we known this was going to go on, we would have stood up a full ASOC [Air Support Operations Center] and moved to Bagram a week or two weeks ahead of this and then conducted a set of rehearsals with carriers, with the bombers, with the whole thing. And I would have forward-deployed the A-10s ..." (Quoted in HQ USAF 2005: 54).

None of the services were yet particularly adjusted to acting on a war footing with the Air Force's ridiculous request to swap over ETACs midway through the battle being just one example. There were also 30-plus ETACs, Combat Controllers, and airborne FACs in the battlespace, which contributed greatly to the de-confliction chaos.

Dissemination of battlefield intelligence suffered as key information appeared not to be available to all participants. The CIA, the AFO, and the Special Forces openly shared information and attempted to facilitate a similar level of cooperation with the conventional forces. Vital AFO intelligence, which indicated that the enemy was dug in using prepared positions on the ridges surrounding the valley and not inhabiting the villages on the valley floor, was passed on to Task Force Rakkasan but was not acted upon because it was considered "too late" to modify at the eleventh hour.

Based on the early intelligence that Afghan civilians still lived in the four villages (Serkhankheyl, Babukhel, Marzak, and Zerkekale) in the Rakkasans' AO, restrictive rules of engagement were in place to minimize potential civilian casualties. This led to the conventional ground forces initially considering the mission as one of "sweep and clear" rather than the high-intensity meeting engagement that it became. Had the intelligence been acted upon, Task Force Rakkasan would have entered the fight more prepared in terms of both equipment and tactics.

A Fairchild Republic A-10A Thunderbolt II, known as the Warthog from its less than pleasing aesthetics, sits on the strip at Bagram Air Base. The Warthog was introduced late into the battle and flew top cover for the extraction helicopters on March 4. (DOD)

Some commentators have also questioned the decision of Task Force Rakkasan to not bring their 105mm field artillery with them, instead relying on limited 60mm, 81mm, and 120mm organic fires and Apache cover. Staff officers within both the 10th Mountain and 101st Airborne defend their decision as the tactical picture at the time indicated that integral mortar support, along with the Apaches would suffice. A very reasoned argument can be made against sling-loaded 105mm artillery pieces under Chinooks being flown into mountainous areas with a largely unknown air-defense threat.

Close air support was also sometimes less than optimal. The Air Force had little recent experience in supporting friendly forces on an asymmetric battlefield. Control of CAS proved difficult as the USAF no longer had any specialist platforms to command and control air support to ground troops in contact. Instead they were forced to rely upon AWACS and JSTARS, two platforms that were not designed for this purpose. The situation later improved with liaisons from both conventional and SOF serving with the aircrews.

Although CAS missions should be controlled by forward observers embedded with ground forces, the Air Force command in Saudi Arabia aborted some CAS strikes as they attempted to control all operations in the airspace. Of no help were the tremendous number of air assets that increasingly entered the airspace above the Shahikot. Army Apaches and later Marine Cobras, CIA Predators, A-10 tank-busters, and Air Force, Marine, and Navy fast jets all added to the air control and de-confliction nightmare. Many of these difficulties thankfully had been overcome by the conclusion of the operation, principally by bringing the air component command "into the picture."

Despite these difficulties, an Air Force report noted that fast air CAS delivered 177 JDAM and GBU-12 bombs during the first full day of operations alone – 162 of these were in support of troops in contact or guided by the SOF teams. Some 750 bombs were delivered in the first three days – a number that goes against some of the criticism of the air support provided.

One other CAS success story from *Anaconda* was the tenacity and bravery shown by the aviators of the Killer Spades in their AH-64A Apaches. Despite multiple RPG strikes, near-misses, and airbursts, and being peppered by small-arms and antiaircraft machine-gun fire, the Killer Spades continued to provide vital close air support. The fact they flew the older-model AH-64A also proved a blessing in disguise as the newer AH-64D with the rotor-mounted Longbow radar was significantly heavier and may have struggled in the thin air of the mountains.

The Task Force Rakkasan soldiers fighting on the valley floor suffered in a similar way to the SEALs and Rangers on Takur Ghar due to their short-barreled 5.56mm carbines. In the valley, this deficiency was made worse by the long ranges involved. Lester Grau has noted that upon the initial insertion, the heavier-caliber M240 machine guns, M24 sniper rifles, and .50-caliber McMillan antimaterial rifles carried by the Canadian forces were the only weapons systems that could effectively reach the enemy.

Experiences like this in the early days of both the Afghan and Iraq campaigns led to the concept of the Designated Marksman in many Coalition armies. This marksman is generally equipped with a semiautomatic 7.62mm rifle and magnified optics that can reach out farther than the carbines and rifles carried by most members of an infantry platoon. Designated Marksmen are now often assigned at the section/squad level. Squad automatic weapons in 7.62mm caliber, enhanced grenade launchers such as the M32, M320, and the futuristic XM-25, and sniper rifles chambered for the long-range .338 have also been introduced since *Anaconda* to provide a longer-range capability in the infantry fight.

Of all the issues highlighted, the most impactful on both the battle for Takur Ghar and the wider *Anaconda* effort, was one of confused command and control. Decisions that affected the lives of the troops on the ground were made with limited understanding and appreciation of the battlespace. Tactical decisions were apparently made by staff officers far removed from the physical battlefield. Initially, conventional forces, Air Force, and "white" SOF were under separate commands that did little to improve coordination and planning. The fact that Task Force 11 remained under a separate command also added to the difficulties when its members ran into trouble on Takur Ghar.

Despite the numerous difficulties, Operation *Anaconda* can and should be considered a success. US forces adapted and overcame numerous obstacles and it is doubtful whether a less professional military force could have done so. The SEALs and Rangers on Takur Ghar also managed to prevail in extremely trying conditions – another testament to their bravery and resourcefulness. Special operations planning and command and control have been significantly overhauled and improved upon since March 2002. Likewise, coordination between conventional forces, SOF, and the Air Force has developed into a far more cohesive whole through the grim experience of both Afghanistan and Iraq.

A designated marksman of the 3rd Battalion, 187th Infantry provides overwatch to his comrades during Operation *Mountain Lion*, the follow-up sweep after *Anaconda*. This soldier has apparently mounted a commercial telescopic 'scope to the carrying handle of his M4 carbine. (US Army)

BIBLIOGRAPHY

All of these works have proved useful, but for a deeper understanding of particular aspects of the battle of Takur Ghar and the larger Operation *Anaconda* itself, I would highlight the following: Sean Naylor's *Not a Good Day to Die*, offering an excellent overview of the battle from an SOF perspective; Malcolm Macpherson's *Roberts Ridge*, which adds significant detail primarily from the perspective of the SEALs of MAKO 30; Peter Blaber's *The Mission, the Men, and Me* for the Delta/AFO perspective; Nate Self's *Two Wars*, which provides an amazing first-person account of the battle from the leader of the Ranger QRF; and finally Lester Grau and Dodge Billingsley's *Operation Anaconda*, which has fast become the definitive source on *Anaconda*.

Australian Defence Force Special Operations Command (2002). "Australia's commitment to the coalition against terrorism including an update on operation Anaconda." <www.defence.gov.au/media/2002/0803200202.doc> (accessed August 1, 2012).

Bay, Austin (2002). "A Full Report on Operation Anaconda – America's First Battle of the 21st Century. A Complete After Action Interview with COL Wiercinski." <http://www.strategypage.com/on_point/20020627.aspx> (accessed August 1, 2012).

Blaber, Peter (2008). *The Mission, the Men, and Me*. New York, NY: Berkley Caliber.

Briscoe, Charles H., Richard L. Kiper, James A. Schroder & Kalev I. Sepp (2003). *Weapon of Choice: US Army Special Operations Forces in Afghanistan*. Fort Leavenworth, Kansas: Combat Studies Institute Press.

Camp, Dick (2011). *Boots On The Ground: The Fight to Liberate Afghanistan from Al-Qaeda and the Taliban 2001–2002*. Minneapolis, MN: Zenith Press.

Crosby, Ron (2009). *NZSAS: The First Fifty Years*. Auckland: Penguin.

Durant, Michael J. & Steven Hartow (2008). *The Night Stalkers: Top Secret Missions of the U.S. Army's Special Operations Aviation Regiment*. New York, NY: NAL Caliber.

Graham, Bradley (2002). "Bravery and Breakdowns in a Ridgetop Battle." <http://www.washingtonpost.com/wp-dyn/articles/A1951-2002May23_4.html> (accessed August 1, 2012).

Grau, Lester W. & Dodge Billingsley (2011). *Operation Anaconda: America's First Major Battle In Afghanistan*. Lawrence, KA: University Press of Kansas.

Headquarters, United States Air Force (2005). "Operation Anaconda – An Air Power Perspective." <http://www.af.mil/shared/media/document/AFD-060726-037.pdf> (accessed August 1, 2012).

Hirsch, Michael (2003). *None Braver: U.S. Air Force Pararescuemen in the War on Terrorism*. New York, NY: New American Library.

McElroy, Robert H. (2002). "Afghanistan: Fire Support for Operation Anaconda." *Field Artillery: A Joint Magazine for US Field Artillerymen*, September–October 2002, 5–9.

Macpherson, Malcolm (2005). *Roberts Ridge*. London: Bantam Press.

Maloney, Sean M. (2005). *Enduring The Freedom: A Rogue Historian In Afghanistan*. Washington, DC: Potomac Books.

Naylor, Sean (2005). *Not A Good Day To Die: The Untold Story Of Operation Anaconda*. New York, NY: Berkley Caliber.

Neville, Leigh (2008). *Special Operations Forces in Afghanistan*. Oxford: Osprey.

Self, Nate (2008). *Two Wars: One Hero's Fight On Two Fronts – Abroad and Within*. Carol Stream, IL: Tyndale.

US Department of Defense (2003). Joint Publication 3-05, *Doctrine for Joint Special Operations* (Washington, DC).

INDEX